RADIO CONTROL
FOAM
MODELLING

David Thomas

Revised
Sid King

www.specialinterestmodelbooks.co.uk

Special Interest Model Books Ltd.
P.O. Box 327
Poole
Dorset
BH15 2RG

First published by Argus Books 1989
Reprinted 1994
Revised edition 1999
Reprinted 2010, 2013

ISBN 978-185486-179-5

Printed and bound in Malta by Melita Press

CONTENTS

INTRODUCTION

R/C model airplanes have been around for quite a while and, as the hobby has evolved, so has the use of materials other than the traditional spruce, balsa and plywood. One relatively recent addition to the range has been foam or, to be more precise, expanded polystyrene foam, together with its up-market relation, Styrofoam, more commonly known as blue foam.

It must be said straight away that, as a modelling material, foam suffers from a rather ambiguous reputation. It is considered by some as not being a 'proper' modelling material. Why this should be is rather puzzling, but there is a strong possibility that it stems from the fact that a lot of people just don't know how to use foam, or have had troubles with it. Hence this book, which will attempt to lay down the ground rules for working foam, and also for supplying ideas concerning the uses to which it can be put.

Another reason for this poor reputation may be that modellers believe that foam means heavier models; and, as everyone knows, weight is the common enemy. That this is patently untrue can easily be seen when we look at some of the latest state-of-the-art models, such as ARTF kits and all-foam electric models, where weight is of

This traditional sports trainer features foam wings - simple lines throughout would adapt to all-foam constructions described by the author.

Two-metre sailplane, designed for fast towing and high speed, relies on foam wing not only for strength but also accuracy of aerofoil section. Smooth, efficient and easily produced.

prime importance. Foam does not make for heavier models, if it is used correctly, and the purpose of this book is to show how foam can be used, either as a basic building material, or as a supplement to the more traditional wood structures.

Yet another objection to foam is the belief that, in order to have a foam-cored wing it is necessary to buy it from a specialist manufacturer, which takes a lot of satisfaction out of the hobby. Nothing could be further from the truth; in fact, a great deal of satisfaction can be obtained by making one's own foam wings which will be light, strong, easily repaired and relatively cheap.

Foam is only a base material: by itself it is weak and fragile, but when covered with a suitable skin, it becomes quite strong. It is easily worked, all the more so as it has no grain. It can be cut, both with a hot wire cutter and the ordinary modelling knife, and it can be sanded into quite complex shapes. This means that the number of areas where it can be used are just about limitless.

As far as tools for working it are concerned, the only special one is the hot-wire cutter, and this can be constructed very simply and cheaply by anyone. There are no special glues to be obtained, and the skinning materials are easily available.

In other words, once you gain some familiarity with the medium, working with foam is neither difficult nor unprofitable. There is an added bonus; once you have learnt to handle foam, you will find that you have suddenly become very popular with your fellow modellers - for the simple reason that you are now in a position to do things that they are unable to!

I hope that this book will encourage more modellers to have a go at using foam, and that it will also help others who have already tried, but who have encountered difficulties.

1. BASICS

Which to use?

First, we have to take a look at the types of foam available. Basically there are two, known as white and blue foam, and they are quite different in structure and in use. White polystyrene is the most commonly used foam. Quite simply, this consists of a multitude of small white beads of foam, from 1.5mm to 4mm in diameter, which are heated and formed into sheets in large presses. This foam is not produced for modellers, but for the building trade, where it is used for insulating purposes. There are many different grades. It is usually sold in sheets, about 8 x 4ft, and in various thicknesses. For a beginner, 2 or 2Æin is a suitable size. Don't be put off by the fact that you have to buy a whole sheet. You will find that it is quickly used up.

Just what grade you buy is not too important, but it is better to go for the lighter ones. Naturally, it is difficult to weigh foam sheets at the building stores, so it is better to simply feel the foam. You should look for one that gives a little when you squeeze it, but which is not really soft. It must be borne in mind that the foam itself has very little strength. In the model, this will come from the covering, or skin, as we shall see later.

Avoid recycled foam, since this often contains hard spots caused by the recycled materials, which can deflect or slow-down the cutting wire. Of course, the building merchant may not know if his stock is recycled or not. However, the sheets will themselves have been cut with a hot wire. Careful examination of the surface will reveal the presence of any hard spots showing above the surface, usually a denser white in colour, with 'twang' marks where the wire has been temporarily stalled.

A second source of supply is from those firms which specialise in making foam wings for the model trade, and you will often see their advertisements in the model magazines. This will probably be a little more expensive but the quality will also be higher - it's swings and roundabouts. Another possible source is your local

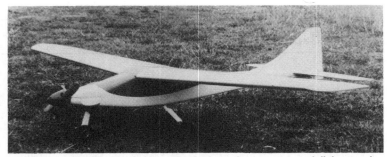

The Metcalfe Models Moonraker, a typical, modern sports modell, has a wing of white foam skinned with obechi.

refrigeration engineer, preferably one that builds cold rooms in butchers' shops and food processors'.

When buying a large sheet, go armed with cutting equipment to avoid transport problems. All you need is a cutter with a new blade, a 4ft straight edge, preferably metallic, such as a piece of aluminium angle, and a measure. Since most people, especially beginners, are not likely to build wings over 6ft span, the best way to cut up an 8ft sheet is probably into two pieces of 3 x 4ft, and one of 2 x 4ft, which should fit quite easily into even a small family car. If you want to build bigger wings, you will have to plan the cutting before you go, although it is quite possible, and sometimes even preferable, to use two pieces of foam to make one half-wing.

When you use the cutter on the foam sheet, you will notice that the resulting cut is rather jagged. Don't worry - it will be tidied up later with the hot wire cutter (HWC). Make several passes using a slicing movement and with a shallow angle between the foam and the blade. This means the cutting edge will be doing most of the work, and not the point, which tends to tear the foam.

The second type of foam available to us is commonly called blue foam. This is quite different in chemical composition, structure, weight and use. It looks different because it consists of millions of tightly-packed fibres instead of beads. This means it is quite a bit heavier than the white variety, so we have to use it for specific applications, where strength is a requirement. Because of its fibrous texture, blue foam can be compared to a very soft wood, but without any grain, and it is thus very easy to work, especially if it has to be sanded. Unless very little pressure is used sandpaper will tend to tear chunks out of white foam, whereas blue is much more resistant. A recent arrival on the foam

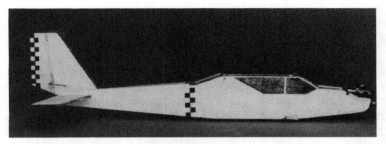

The fuselage of this sport model, which has several years of service behind it, is made entirely from 6mm foamboard - a most versatile material.

scene has been pink foam, a smoother type of styrene foam. This is a closed-cell type of extruded material with a definite skin. I have since come across similar foams in both green and yellow varieties.

These foams are heavier than white foam and less rigid than blue. Possible uses for our purpose would be small flying surfaces, covered with epoxy glass (eliminating the veneer). It has, however, been adopted by the 'indoor flyers', who carve delicate and very thin scale fuselage shells from it.

Another kind of foam is foamboard (Fomecore, in the USA). This is sold in sheets 3 or 6mm thick, and is covered with thin card on both sides. It is light and strong, and can be used as a substitute for balsa, but it does not really come within the scope of this chapter.

There is also a two-part foam mix that can be found in the majority of Do-it-Yourself (DIY) shops, used for filling cavities in walls. This is of no use to us and should be left well alone.

Choice of foam

Three criteria govern the choice of foam to be used namely, price, weight and application. Let's take them in order. White foam is quite a lot cheaper than blue, so this is the first choice from a strictly financial point of view. Weight is an important consideration in most models; here again, white foam has an advantage in that it is around half the weight of blue. As the largest quantity of foam will be in the model's wing core, it is obvious that the lighter that core is, the better the plane will fly, all other things being equal.

So where do we use blue foam? Here we enter the domain of high-performance gliders with medium to heavy wing-loadings, and which are subjected to very high stress in 'ping' winch launches. In this case, the compressibility factor of the core is important, and since blue foam is much more robust than white, it is used almost exclusively for this type of wing.

White foam is generally used for parts of the fuselage which can be made with the HWC, as opposed to shaping by sanding, and which are then skinned with wood. Again, they will be light and cheap. Whilst on the subject, the whole fuselage can be made from foam in this way, and here again, except for really complicated forms, where a lot of sanding is necessary, white foam is quite good enough.

Many accessories can be made with the help of foam. For example, cowlings, undercarriage spats, gun-blisters and even cockpit canopies, as we shall see later on. These are very complicated, rounded shapes, but they are also quite small, so do not require a great deal of material. The easier-to-shape blue foam is preferred here.

To sum up: white foam will do for most jobs, and blue is used for high-stress applications and accessories.

To obtain the best results from white foam, an understanding of its nature is advantageous. A product of the petro-chemical industry, it starts life in granular form, looking like a rather discoloured granulated sugar. The initial expansion takes place by passing the granules through a steam chamber. A measured quantity of semi-expanded beads is then fed into the final mould. Moulds vary in size and shape, perhaps the corner unit in a packing case, a complete model "Spitfire" airframe, or in our case a large steel rectangular chamber. The entire surfaces of the moulds are perforated (1.5mm holes at 300mm spacing).

Once the moulds are closed, super-heated steam is passed through the beads, causing the final expansion, surplus steam exiting via the perforations. The quantity of beads governs the final density of the block, both in terms of weight and the adhesion of one bead to its neighbours.

All very straightforward, and someone else is doing it for us anyway. So how does this knowledge improve our wings? Well firstly it tells us the questions to ask, 'has any recycled 'crumb' been added in the moulding stage?' And 'can I have 16 oz per cu ft virgin bead?' (20oz for 'special' pylon racer or glider wings). If the answer to the former is 'no' and the latter 'yes' you have what you are looking for.

Most specialist suppliers can supply this information. Also, if you have the choice, opt for a fire retardant variety. A little more expensive, but I have seen some very primitive heating arrangements in modellers workshops and polystyrene is very flammable!

The most vital point in understanding foam is that the steaming process leaves residual moisture in the block satisfactory wings will be much easier to produce when the block has dried out naturally.

The drying process can take some considerable time, depending on ambient temperature and humidity. As a rough guide, at normal room temperature it will take 3-4 days for every inch of thickness. This assumes that the sheets can be stacked to allow free air circulation to both sides. This fact in itself is a good argument for cutting panels from individual sheets (e.g. 2 x 2in sheet dries in 7 days, whereas 1 x 4in sheet would require 14 days).

To identify the presence of moisture, look closely at a cut surface. The moisture, if any, is trapped between the beads as the wire passes through the foam. Any wet patch will cool the wire locally, slowing its overall speed. Consequently the slower moving wire in the dry areas will burn away more foam, leaving a quite perceptible step between the two areas. Examination of the wet areas will also reveal that the individual beads have assumed a concave shape, giving a totally different surface texture.

The wet plateaux can, of course, be sanded off, but your section will have lost its accuracy.

2 TOOLS

The hot wire cutter

It is often believed, quite wrongly, that the hot wire cutter (HWC) needed to cut white foam is a highly complicated piece of equipment requiring considerable capital outlay and a lot of technical knowledge to produce. It is, in fact, a very simple tool. One or two are on the market, but it is probably cheaper, and more satisfying, to make one to suit your own purposes. The necessary materials are easily found. Yet another advantage of the model shown in Fig. 2.1 is that the wire can be put under considerable tension, which is a great help in avoiding wire lag when cutting.

The HWC consists of three main elements; the bow, the wire itself and the power supply. The bow can be made from any cheap, knot-free wood, such as pine or deal. The sketch and photo should be sufficient to allow anyone to make one, but we

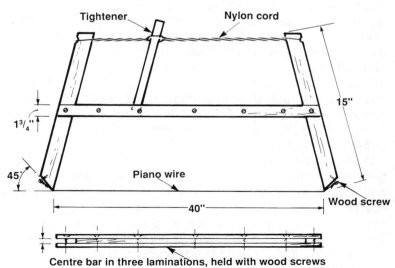

Fig. 2.1 Hot wire cutter

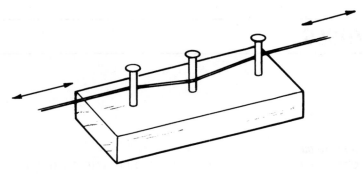

Fig. 2.2 Straightening ni-chrome wire

will emphasise one or two important points.

As shown, the central beam is made from three laminations. This is not absolutely necessary, but it is stronger, and it facilitates the fixing of the two vertical arms. The 45 deg angle at the bottom of these arms should be respected. It allows the HWC to cut right down to about 1mm above the surface on which the foam is laid. This can be very useful. Do not use thinner wood than that specified, because the nylon cord can exert remarkable tension on the device, and if the frame is not strong enough, it will collapse.

The wire is another subject for debate. You may have heard that it is necessary to use ni-chrome or some other exotic material, but whilst it is true that these materials are suitable, they are not indispensable. A good source of ni-chrome is the type of wire used for the elements of electric fires, but it must be new. If you try to unwind the wire from a used bar it will break very easily. Wire taken from an electric fire element, particularly from the 1/4in coil 'spiral' variety will be difficult to pull straight. However, this is easily remedied using a simple tool. Three 75mm nails are driven into a block of wood at 6mm spacing, the block is held firmly in a vice, the wire is then threaded between the nails and pulled back and forwards several times (Fig.2.2).

By far the best material is a length of ordinary stainless steel wire, which can be found in most DIY shops. Choose 0.6mm diameter, or very close to that size, in order to match the power supply. It is simply twisted around the two wood screws at the bottom of the uprights, and then a couple of turns back along itself. In this way, when the HWC is put under tension, the turns will tighten up and prevent the wire slackening.

Power supply

The author's original well-worn HWC (this one does not have the 45 degree subsequently recommended at the bottom of the legs (as mentioned in the text). Note the C of G reference mark in the middle of the bar.

Now to the power supply. The principle of the HWC is that when a low voltage is applied to the wire, it opposes a resistance to the flow of electricity from one end to the other, and that resistance is transformed into heat. It is the heat that allows the HWC to slice through the foam, not by cutting, but by melting it. Obviously, we cannot use the mains supply directly because of the almost certain risk of electrocution. Never apply 240 volts to the HWC, it could be fatal! No, we want a low-voltage supply which poses no danger, and sufficient current to heat the wire. There are several solutions, but the easiest, probably the cheapest, and one that I have used for years, is the common-or-garden car battery charger. It does the job perfectly. Select a model capable of supplying at least 6 amps, preferably 8 amps. A charger with an ammeter is a big advantage, because it will allow you to see just how much current is being drawn, and to adjust it accordingly.

The alternative is to hunt around second-hand electrical shops for a transformer which has a 240 volt input and a 12-15 volt output. The output will be AC, and not DC, as in the case of the battery charger, but this makes absolutely no difference to the performance, and the wiring is the same. However, such transformers are scarce, so the battery charger is probably the easiest solution. If it can be found, by far the best piece of equipment for the purpose is a 'variable transformer' or 'Variac' (Variac is a trade name, but has become a generic term for this equipment). By the simple turning of a calibrated dial, infinitely variable output is possible.

Let's suppose you have opted for a charger, you have made the HWC, and now you want to wire it up (Fig. 2.3). The charger has two leads, one with a plug for the mains supply, and the second terminating in two crocodile clips, one on a black wire, and one on a red. These indicate polarity when hooking up to a car

The power source - an ordinary 6 amp car battery charger. The advantages of this one, which is of French manufacture and fairly old, is that it affords two voltages.

battery, but need not concern us here.

Before plugging in the charger, find a short length of thin, flat wood (say 6in of plywood) and attach the two clips to it, as far from each other as possible. This is to avoid them touching and causing a short circuit. Incidentally, should the clips touch, there will be a fat spark, and the charger's thermal cut-out or fuse will blow. The charger itself will not be damaged, in the normal course of events, but it is obviously better to avoid a short-circuit as there is a slight fire risk. Be very careful not to leave tools near the clips; they too can cause a short. You could even cut short the output leads and fix them to a power socket taped to the charger, thus avoiding any chance of an accident. To connect the power source to the HWC you need about 6ft of ordinary house-hold twin-core electrical cable which should be fairly thick, to avoid power losses due to voltage drop, but again the dimen-

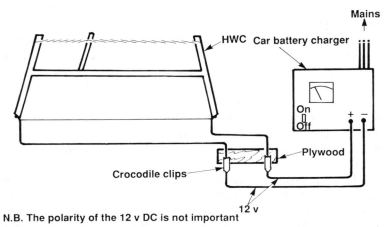

N.B. The polarity of the 12 v DC is not important

Fig. 2.3 HWC power supply hook-up

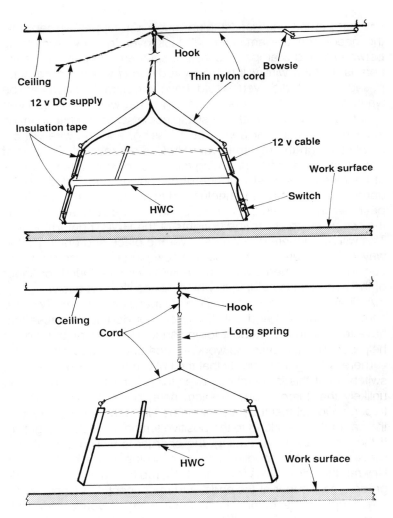

Fig. 2.5 Spring suspension

sions are far from critical. While you are at it, buy a small pear switch as used for bedside lamps. Strip about 1/2in of the insulation from both ends of the cable at one extremity, and trap these under the crocodile clips. Strip 1 1/2in of insulation from the other end, and wrap the bared ends around the wire of the HWC, as close to the uprights as possible. Hold the HWC by the centre beam in one hand, making sure that it is not touching anything, and plug in the charger. Nothing much will happen, except that the needle on the ammeter will kick over to show something between 3 and 5 amps. A constant source of surprise to beginners is that the wire will not glow red. Don't worry, it's not supposed to (if it did, you would have problems!). However, be warned; even if there is no visual sign, that wire is hot, so keep your fingers away from it! To test it, place a scrap of white foam on the wire. You will hear a very faint hissing, and the wire will cut slowly through the material; your HWC is operational. Comfort of operation is everything in cutting foam, so you can make a couple of improvements. First, cut one of the power leads, close to the upright - after first having unplugged from the mains! - and fit the pear switch between the cut ends. Now use electrical tape to fix the two wires solidly to the uprights of the HWC, right to the top. This will avoid them dangling all over the place and getting in the way while you are cutting. You can now plug in the charger when setting up, and then switch on the HWC with the thumb or finger of the hand that is holding it, which makes life a lot easier.

A final improvement is to fit a suspension system. Two are shown in Figs. 2.3 and 2.4. If you cannot do this, because you have to work in the kitchen, for instance, don't worry, but it does help because it leaves the working area unencumbered.

There is a slight possibility that the HWC may not work when you switch on. If this is so, check everything. First the charger - it is unlikely that there is any problem here, but some duds do get through. Do not test it by touching one clip with the other; try it on the car battery, red lead to the positive terminal, black to negative. If the meter shows a reading, the charger is working. Jiggle the wires under the crocodile clips, in case there is a bad contact. Unwrap the bared wires from the HWC, rub the cutter wire with 600 grade emery paper at the ends, and re-connect. It will now work.

A couple more points. First, don't worry if you accidentally touch the wire while the HWC is switched on. In the first place, it is at 12 volts, the same as your car battery, so there is absolutely no chance of getting a shock. Secondly, the wire is hot, but a fleeting contact will not cause a burn. That does not mean that you should not be careful, but the danger is fairly slight. However, it is quite hot enough to cut foam, even if that wire is not glowing.

Finally, store your HWC under tension where it is not likely to be damaged. It is not particularly fragile, but breakage, or a kink in the wire, is to be avoided. Remember, the transformer or Variac must be disconnected from the mains when not in use.

Alternative bow construction

Having described the traditional bow, inasmuch as a 30-year-old method can be said to be traditional (although it is based on the very traditional bow saw) there is a simpler type. The 'simple bow' consists of a rigid beam of 50 x 25mm timber (for bows up to 1 metre) or 60 x 30mm for bows of around 1-1.5 metres. Inserted into the ends of the beam are 2 x 450mm lengths of 6 swg piano wire spread outwards at 20 deg from the vertical (F2.5) the ends of the wires being 'necked' to receive the cutting wire.

The ni-chrome wire is secured to one leg by making three turns around the 'neck' and making off around itself, the wire is then tensioned by pushing the leg that has already received the wire against a suitable wall or bench top and securing the wire to the second leg.

Electrical connections are made by soldering the two supply cables to the protruding ends of the legs, the 'long' cable being secured to the beam with tape. As an extra precaution to keep the supply cables clear of the cutting wire (should the two meet when 'live', the results are spectacular!) use a 300mm piece of 18 swg piano wire as a flexible stand-off support. To the regular user the 'simple bow' has many advantages:-

1. If prolonged use is envisaged, it is much lighter to handle, the bigger bows have lightening holes cut along their length.
2. Its quick construction enables a range of bows to match specific tasks - (I have 14 from 1-1.5 metres).

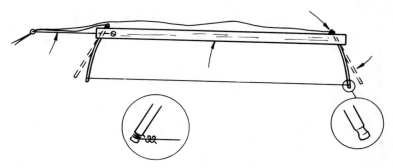

Fig. 2.6 Alternative bow construction

3. They are more convenient, being held by the beam, for one-person operation - see later chapter on 'single handed cutting'.

3 TEMPLATES

Aerofoil guides

It must be understood, right from the start, that templates are necessary. They serve as guides for the HWC, in order to reproduce accurately the aerofoil required. Without them, the wire will wander all over the place as it cuts the foam. As an experiment, draw a curved line on a scrap of foam, switch on the HWC and try to cut along the line - accurately. Point taken?

The principle of cutting foam cores is to take a block of foam, fix the templates to each end and then run the HWC across the edges of the two templates. The path the HWC takes is thus dictated by the shape of the templates, and the result is a piece of foam cut to exactly the same shape.

The aerofoil section will depend on the plane you want to build. Essentially, there are three sources. Firstly, you may wish to replace a broken wing on an existing model. In this case you can use the broken wing, cut cleanly across the chord, to take a tracing of the aerofoil - not forgetting to make allowances for the thickness of the skin. Secondly, you can take a tracing from a plan and finally, you can use ordinate tables, which will allow you to draw up the exact chord you require (see the chapter on Aerofoils). You can, of course, invent your own but, unless you have a lot of experience in this field, don't bother; it will never be as efficient as a properly designed one.

The material to be used for the templates can be plywood, aluminium sheet or Formica. The plywood should be 2-3mm in thickness, and of good quality. If it is cheap, fibrous wood, there is a danger of the HWC catching in the fibres and causing imperfections in the core. If aluminium is used, it should not be more than 1mm thick, or it will absorb heat from the wire, causing uneven local cutting. Formica is ideal, particularly if you can find a source of off-cuts.

There are two types of template, a single and double (Fig. 3.1). Which to use? The single template is quicker and cheaper to pro-

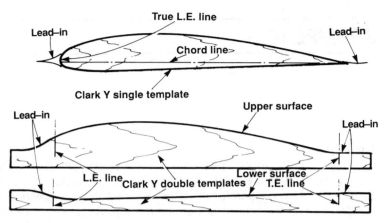

Fig. 3.1 Single and double templates

duce, but there is a disadvantage, particularly for beginners to foam cutting. At first there is a definite tendency to press the HWC down a little too hard on the template - a quite natural action. Under this pressure, there is a danger that the nails used to attach the template will move in the foam, which is a relatively soft material, and the result will be that the template will move a little, thus producing an inaccurate core. However, we must not exaggerate, for many modellers use this type of template without any problems. The double template is more expensive in material costs and takes longer to make, but, as it sits with its bottom edge on the work surface, the amount of pressure put on it is immaterial because it cannot move vertically, and it is for this reason that I would advise any beginner to use it. I never use anything else now, in the interests of accuracy.

Let's take a closer look at the single template. Having chosen the material, draw or trace your aerofoil onto it, and then add the chord line in heavy pencil. Next a controversial point - whether or not to use a 'lead-in' for the HWC. If your wing has a separate leading edge spar, there is no problem; draw a lead-in as shown. If, on the other hand, you want to try a wrap-around skin instead of a separate leading edge - not really recommended for beginners - then omit it. In this case the cutting operation will have to be modified slightly, as we shall see.

When you are satisfied that you have an accurate outline, cut out the template, taking care to keep the cut just outside the drawn line. Finish off by sanding down to the line with succes-

Fig. 3.2 Template edge
bevelled

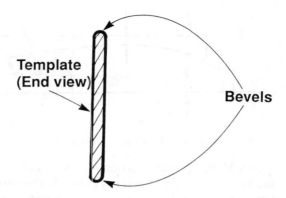

**Template
(End view)**

Bevels

sively finer grades of sandpaper, terminating with 400 grade emery, used dry. The edges of the template must be absolutely smooth, because any imperfection will be reproduced on the surface of the foam core. It is also as well to bevel the edges slightly, in order to reduce the drag of the HWC (Fig. 3.2). The last task is to drill holes to take the thin nails which will be used to fix the template to the foam block.

The double template takes a little more planning. Let us suppose that you want to cut a Clark Y aerofoil from a block of foam 2in thick. You will need two pieces of template material, each about 2in longer than the chord of the panel to be cut. Mark the bottom edges with a pencil, and then sand them absolutely flat.

Next, you will have to work out where the chord line is to come, with respect to this bottom edge, in order to ensure that the aerofoil will be centred vertically in the foam block (Fig. 3.3). In other words, there should be as much surplus material above the aerofoil as there is below it. As an example, let us say that the chord

The two different types of template mentioned in the text. The upper one is a single template; the lower sets are doubles.

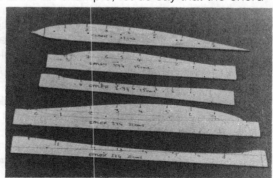

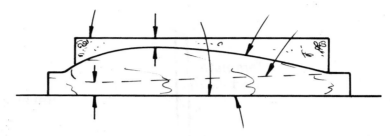

Fig. 3.3 Placing double template on foam block

line is 3/4in. up from the bottom. Draw in this chord line on both pieces of template material, parallel to the sanded bottom edge. Draw a vertical line about 1in from one end, measure off the exact length of the aerofoil, and draw a second vertical line at this point. Now draw the upper surface of the aerofoil between these two vertical lines, including a lead-in if necessary. Do exactly the same on the second piece, but this time draw the lower surface. You can now cut them out and finish them in the same way as for the single template.

In both cases you will need root and tip templates. In the case of a parallel wing they will be identical but, if you are making a tapered wing, the tip template will obviously be smaller.

Cutting the blocks

Having made the templates, it is now necessary to cut up two blocks of foam in order to produce the wing panels. This is a most important process, and one that should not be hurried, because a properly-cut block is essential to create an accurate core. Since a purely theoretical explanation is difficult to follow, we will take a concrete example; and to make life even simpler, we will consider the building of a wing that is suitable both for a 3.5cc trainer and a basic slope soarer. Our choice is a 50in span wing of parallel planform with a 7in Clark Y aerofoil.

To cut vertical sides on the blocks, a couple of set-squares are needed, made from plywood and with 1 1/2in rails glued and screwed to the bottom edges so that they can be screwed or clamped to the work surface (Fig. 3.4). Make them at least 6in high so they can be used later for sizing up thicker blocks of foam, such as those made up for cowls. If you intend to cut a good deal of foam, you will need a simple, but quite invaluable accessory - the sizing board, or jig (Fig. 3.5). Make this from a

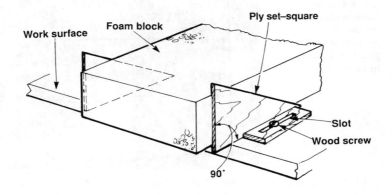

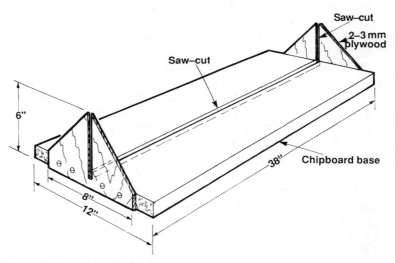

Fig. 3.5 Foam block cutting jig

piece of fairly thick chipboard, or similar material, of about 38 x
l2in though you should check the length against your HWC, to
make sure that the latter will clear the end-pieces. Draw a line
lengthwise at the centre of this board, and then cut a groove
along it with an electric saw, such that the depth of the groove is
about half the thickness of the wood.

Next, cut out two triangles about 6in high from a piece of 2-
3mm plywood, and make a vertical cut in each with a fine hacksaw blade. This cut must be absolutely straight, because it will

A sheet of white foam in place on the block-cutting jig, with the HWC positioned ready to slice it up.

be the guide for the wire. Now screw the two triangles to the board, so that the cuts in the triangle and the board are all in line. Place the wire of the HWC in the two guides, and slide it down - it should disappear into the groove in the board. This means that during cutting, the wire will cut right through the block without stopping short of the bottom surface.

With an ordinary cutter and straight edge, chop up two blocks of foam about 27 x 9in. Cut the edges as straight as possible, but don't worry too much if they are a bit jagged.

Fix the two set-squares to the work surface, some 36in apart, in such a way that the vertical edges overhang by 1/2in Place the block of foam between them, this time with one long edge over-hanging by 1 1/2in Place a flat piece of wood, approximately 24 x 3in on the foam and place weights on top - 4-5lbs will do - this will keep the block in place, and will be used in the actual core-cutting. Holding the HWC by the centre beam, switch it on and wait about 15 seconds for it to warm up. Then place the wire against the two set-squares, above the foam block, and then run it down them, maintaining a gentle pressure against them, until the wire reaches the foam. Here we come to what is probably the most important point in cutting foam in this way; do not force the cut. Let the wire move through the foam at its own speed. If you start forcing it now, you will continue to do so when cutting the core, and this will cause defects. The weight of the HWC is quite sufficient to take it down and out of the bottom of the block.

Remember, the wire is not really cutting the foam, it is melting its way through. Don't worry about the fact that the movement is slow. This is a function of the temperature of the wire, which is not high.

When this first cut has been made, turn the block through 180 deg and measure off 7in from the cut edge, at each end of the block. Mark these points with a felt-tipped pen. Now, place the HWC, with the power switched off, so that the wire lies across the two pen marks. Gently push the foam block back until the wire just makes contact with the edges of the set-squares. Switch on, and cut the second side.

Turn the block so that one short end is overhanging. Draw a line 1in from this end at right-angles to the two cut sides, and cut. Measure up 25in from this end on both sides of the block, make two marks, turn the block round and go through the same operation as for the second long cut. You will now have a foam block with perfectly vertical sides, cut to the exact dimensions you require to make a wing panel. Do exactly the same with the second block.

Of course, the foregoing assumes two things. Firstly, that we are cutting blocks for a parallel wing. If it is a tapered wing, the best solution is to draw a centre-line with the felt pen on top of the block, and then mark out the four edges to be cut using this as a reference line (Fig. 3.6). It is not difficult, it just requires a bit of common sense.

The second supposition is that we are cutting the complete chord. However, if, as I suggest, you make your first attempt on a wing with a separate leading-edge spar, your block would not be 7in wide, but 6 1/2in supposing that the LE spar is 1/2in thick.

The next step is of the utmost importance, since it is designed to avoid the 'two-left-hand-panels' syndrome, probably the most annoying - and common - mistake committed when making foam-cored wings. Place the two blocks on the work-surface, with their root ends touching, so that they create the planform of the final wing.

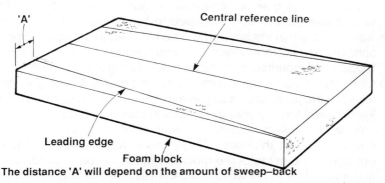

The distance 'A' will depend on the amount of sweep–back

Fig. 3.6 Marking-out block for tapered wing panel

If the blanks are marked like this, there is no danger of cutting identical but non-handed, wing panels.

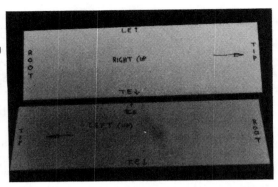

With a felt pen, mark the two touching edges 'root' and the two long edges 'leading edge'. The two extremities should be marked 'tip', and you should now be safe from the syndrome - if, of course, you check to see what is written on the blocks before cutting! If you want to be absolutely sure, mark them 'right-up' and 'left-up' respectively (Fig. 3.7). It may seem like over-kill, but at least you will end up with two usable cores! Now that the blocks are sized up, the last thing that remains to be done is to fix the templates to the two ends of one block. In the case of the single template, this requires marking the block with a line, drawn by the felt pen, all round the sides of the block. In the case of a wing with no washout, this is easy. The line will be 3/4in up from the bottom, and parallel to it. If the panel needs some washout, say 3 deg, draw a line on the trailing edge side of the block at that angle to the base. When the line reaches the tip, it will be quite a bit higher than the original line (Fig. 3.8). The line across the tip must then drop from this point to join the leading edge line.

If you are using single templates an absolute necessity is a flat work-board, as the work will need to be turned over, any span-wise curvature in the surface will be mirrored in the reverse position, giving rise to inconsistent wing thickness - mine is 25mm blockboard mounted on a frame welded from 25mm square steel tube, the board being shimmed with pieces of 0.4mm ply to give a level surface. A good alternative board is a piece of rolled edge kitchen worktop, try your local kitchen fitter for off-cuts.

A natural assumption is that your sheet of foam is both flat and of constant thickness. Sadly this is not always so. Sheets cut from the outside of the moulded block will often be distinctly curved. This is because uneven pressures during expansion give rise to internal tensions, which are released when the sheet

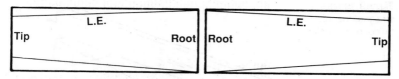

Fig. 3.7 Avoiding two left wing panels

is cut. No amount of bending in the opposite direction will cure this condition.

We are left with two options: either to hold the sheet flat during cutting with weights, which invariably means that the wing will adopt the original curvature when released. This can only complicate the skinning process to say nothing of introducing internal stresses into the finished product which may, in turn, lead to a warp and is a bit of a 'black hat' solution. On the other hand, the guys in the white hats would start with a slightly thicker material and 'skim' the blocks level.

This levelling of the playing field is one of the major factors in producing accurate, stable wings and requires very little time or equipment, the basis of which is two straight edges with a means of adjusting their height above the work surface. A simple straight edge can be made from a selected straight piece of timber of suitable size (say 2 x 1in, 18in long) with a piece of 10 swg piano wire epoxied its surface (Fig.3.9). The top surface of the wire should be clear of epoxy as it will act as a guide for the cutting wire. The two battens can then be adjusted for height by packing pieces under each end. Make these packing pieces in

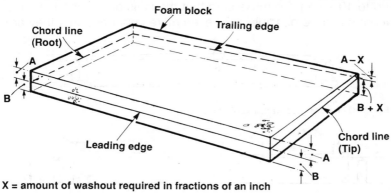

X = amount of washout required in fractions of an inch

Fig. 3.8 Marking washout onto foam block

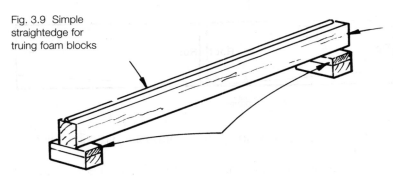

Fig. 3.9 Simple straightedge for truing foam blocks

sets of four as required - say 4 x 1/2, 4 x 1/4 & 4 x 1/8in for a start.

Begin by placing the foam convex side up and holding down with small weights placed only at each end. The purpose of these weights is to stop the foam riding up when the wire passes through, not to bend the foam. Adjust the straight edges to 1/8in below the edge of the block (Fig.3.10) and make the first cut. Now turn the block over and secure with heavy weights. Re-adjusting the height of the cut to 1/8in less than the lowest point in the remaining curvature (Fig.3.11), cut off the unwanted piece and you are left with a stable, accurate wing blank.

You will remember that you have drawn the chord line on the templates. These are now fixed in place, so that this chord line covers the lines you have just drawn on the block. I use 50x3mm 'OBO' masonry nails, sharpened to a needle point. These nails have the advantage of a tapered shank which takes up any slight slack in the template holes, and are of sufficient diameter to give a good grip into the foam. Two are normally adequate for chords up to 10 - 12in. Do make sure that the nails are pushed into the foam as far as possible and, even more important, that they are

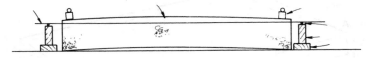

Fig. 3.10 Trimming convex side of foam block

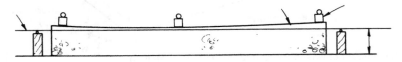

Fig. 3.11 Second cut - trimming concave side of block

Single side template positioned for symmetrical wing cutting.

parallel to the work surface. If they are not, there is a risk of them catching on the HWC during the cut, and causing trouble.

The double templates do not need this marking out. Simply place the two upper surface templates in place against the block ends and fix them. If washout is needed, the trailing edge of the tip template is simply packed up with scrap wood to the required height. However, do make a note of how you do this, so that you can repeat it exactly on the second panel. There is nothing worse than a twisted wing. There is a danger when cutting a fairly thick section, such as a Wortmann, by this method. In this case, the lower template will be very thin in the middle, and if it is packed up, the weight of the HWC may make it bend downwards, thus changing the true shape of the wing section. It is far better to cut the template with the required amount of washout already incorporated - in this way, the whole of the template will remain securely on the work surface, and there will be no danger of bending.

An alternative method of locating single templates was given to me many years ago by Pat French of P.F.M. models. The amount of time it has saved me in the intervening years warrants a spe-

Using straightedges (steel in this instance) as a guide for truing block (Bill Burkinshaw photo)

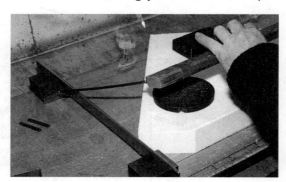

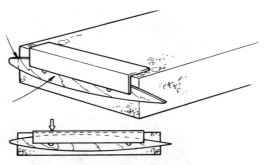

Fig. 3.12 Aligning template using aluminium angle

cial acknowledgement.

No marking out of the centre line is necessary, in its place a piece of aluminium angle is placed over the block of foam (Fig.3.12). The template is loosely held between the aluminium and the foam with the leading edge aligned and the nail holes half exposed. The sharpened OBO nails are then pushed into the holes whilst firmly holding the aluminium against the top of the block. The resultant action automatically lines up the top of the holes in the template with the edge of the aluminium. If you can accumulate a selection of different sized angle pieces you will have a consistent automatic means of alignment.

To introduce wash-out to this arrangement it only remains to off-set the holes in the tip template. Draw a secondary centre line at the washout angle required. A variation of the above method is to use an accurate wooden spacer to locate the required centre line above the board, again using the principle of the half exposed hole (Fig.3.13).

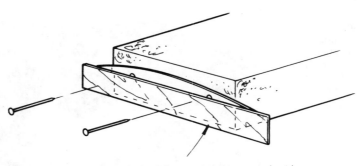

Fig. 3.13 An alternative to the aluminium angle is to use a ply strip

Aluminium angle in use to position template on delta wing foam blank. (Bill Burkenshaw photo)

All the foregoing supposes that the span of the wing is such that you can cut each half-wing in one panel. Obviously, when we come to 4 metre gliders, this is no longer true, particularly when these big models, especially the scale ones, have a double-taper planform. It is obviously impossible to cut such a panel in one go.

No real problem; you will have to use two pieces of foam for each panel, and thus three templates instead of two.

When using this method, two points should be observed. The first is that accurate alignment between the two panels is imperative, especially in height. It thus becomes obvious that double templates are necessary, to prevent inaccuracies caused by movement of the single template. The second point concerns the appearance of the finished model. It is far better to plan and cut the templates in such a way that the upper surface of the wing is a straight line, from root to tip. In this way the diminution in thickness over its length appears on the lower surface, and is less visible, and secondly, this reduction in thickness adds to the effective dihedral of the wing, instead of detracting from it (Fig. 3.14).

When you cut the wing, the centre template will be used twice, first as the tip plate for the inboard section, and secondly as the root plate for the outboard section. The true root and tip templates will be used once each, in the usual way.

4 CUTTING FOAM CORES

Get assistance

Cutting cores needs two pairs of hands. If you have a friend who also wants to make foam wings, he will be ideal, because he has a vested interest in the success of the operation. If not, try and grab someone who is good with his hands.

Before starting, one point has to be understood; the HWC has to move into the foam block parallel to one long edge, and emerge parallel with the other. With a parallel panel this is not a problem, but with a tapered one some way is needed to ensure this happens, otherwise the aerofoil may not be respected along the length of the panel. The solution is to divide the templates up into an equal number of divisions (Fig. 4.1). Mark the centre of each template with felt pen. Now mark the centres of the two halves thus created. Repeat the performance, and the template will be divided into eight equal parts by seven vertical lines. These lines are then numbered 1-7. The block, with the templates in place, is put in the middle of the work surface, and the wooden slat and weights are loaded on top. The two operators place themselves at each end of the block and take the HWC in one hand, holding it low down on the uprights, near the wire.

Before starting, decide who is going to do the calling.

The HWC, still cold, is placed on the lead-in of the trailing edge. With the double template, this is easy. With the single, you will be within a couple of millimetres of the foam, so be careful. No.1, the caller, switches on the HWC, and then waits for it to reach working temperature. On the word 'Go!' both gently push the HWC

Holes for pins or nails

Fig. 4.1 Template divisions for HWC

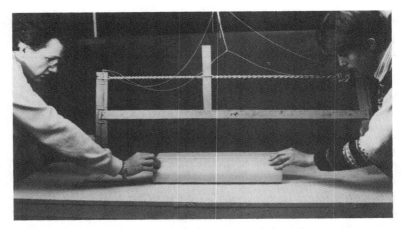

Using theHWC by hand, in this case on a fuselage turtle-deck. The work is being held because it is difficult to place weights on the rounded surface.

Always start the first cut from the brailing edge - in this case the electric cutting unit is being used.

into the foam. Don't force it; remember, you are melting, not cutting, so let it go at its own speed. No.1 concentrates on keeping the HWC moving at a constant speed. When the wire reaches the first mark on the template, he calls out 'One'. No.2 checks if the wire is at that point on his template. If it is not yet there, he must speed up the cutting rate slightly. If it has gone past, he will have to slow down. It is best to have No.2, who is not the caller, cutting the tip, especially on a tapered panel, because it will be easier for him to modulate the cutting speed at this end.

The cut continues. When No.1 reaches the second mark, he calls out 'Two', and No.2 adjusts the cut again. Continue the same process until the wire emerges from the block at the leading edge. The moment it does so, stop its progress, and keep still. No.1 switches off and then inspects the wire. Ideally, there will be dozens of fine, hair-like filaments attached to the wire, running back to the edge of the block. This is a sure indication that the temperature of the wire is about right.

Faults and remedies

Place the HWC on the work-surface, unload the weights and wood slat, lift off the foam off-cut, and take a careful look at the surface you have just created because this is where you have to take stock. If you have a perfectly smooth, matt surface, slightly soft to the touch, without any ridges, you are lucky! To be honest, this occurs only rarely on the first attempt. What is more likely is that the surface has lots of tiny ridges on it. Don't worry; the core is usable, so don't give up yet! There are three possible causes for these ridges. The first is uneven cutting speed, and that is a matter of practice, nothing more. The second reason could be imperfections on the edge of one, or both, of the templates. The test is to run your finger-nail vertically along the edge of the template. If you can feel the slightest imperfection, it is not good enough. Go over it again with some 600 grade emery until you can feel no resistance at all, just your nail sliding smoothly along. The third cause may be uneven pressure of the HWC on the templates. If you have used double templates, this shouldn't happen, because you can afford to put a reasonable amount of pressure on them, and they cannot move because they are sitting on the work surface. It is trickier where the single template is used, because too much pressure will tear the nails through the foam, allowing the template to move, whilst not enough pressure may allow the HWC to lift slightly, leaving a ridge.

A second fault may be that instead of a soft, matt surface you find a very hard, granulated one. This is because the cut was too slow, or the wire too hot - the two factors are obviously interrelat-

A template with a defect in its edge has caused these ridges in the core.

ed. If you have kept a light and constant pressure on the HWC then the cutting speed was probably right. If, on the other hand, the ammeter reading is high, that is, over 5 amps, reduce the temperature of the wire. Go to a lower setting if you are lucky enough to have a charger which you can adjust. Choose a lower voltage if you have a transformer with a series of output tappings.

If you can do neither of these things, there are still two solutions. Either change the resistance of the wire (in this case by using a slightly thinner one) or, and this is the better choice, modify the HWC. To do this, you will need another length of wire, almost twice the length of the original one. Fit it to the HWC in the usual way, which means that you will have a long length over. This should be formed around a piece of dowel or a pencil to make a coil. Ensure that the turns are not touching one another. This coil is fitted inside the angle between the taut wire and the upright (Fig. 4.2).

Fit the power lead from the charger with a miniature crocodile clip. By moving this up or down the coil, you will find that you can adjust the temperature of the HWC, because you are in fact changing the effective length of the wire, and thus its resistance.

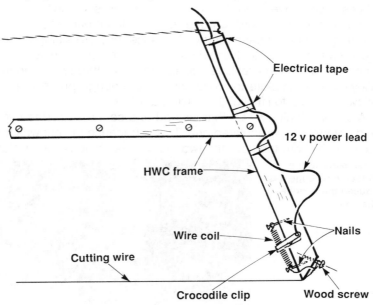

Fig. 4.2 HWC temperature adjuster coil

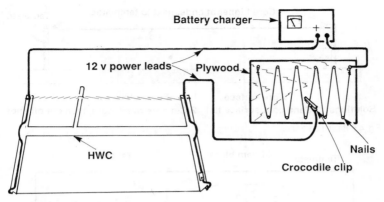

Fig. 4.3 Remote HWC temperature control

Keep your fingers away from the coil, because the lower part will reach the same temperature as the wire used for melting the foam. A remote version is shown in Fig. 4.3. From there on, it is a case of experimenting to find the best temperature (now you can see how you can get through a whole sheet of foam when you begin cutting foam!).

You may find another fault. If you sight spanwise along the cut surface you may notice a distinct hollow in it. This comes from wire lag (Fig. 4.4). Pushing the HWC too fast through the foam will cause the centre of the wire to trail behind the two ends, not only horizontally but also vertically, thanks to the force of gravity. The answer is to check the tension of the HWC. You should get a high-pitched 'Ping!' from the wire when it is plucked. If not, tighten it up a little, but go carefully. The pressure exerted is high. Secondly, slow down the cutting rate.

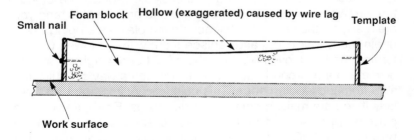

Fig. 4.4 Hollow in core due to wire lage

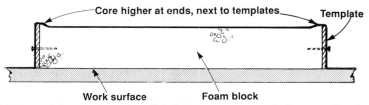

Core higher at ends, next to templates — Template

Work surface   Foam block

Solutions: 1. Sand core surface flat   2. Cut core overlength, then cut off ends

Fig. 4.5 Raised core ends

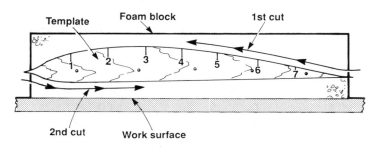

Template   Foam block   1st cut

2nd cut   Work surface

Fig. 4.6 Core cutting sequence

If you are observant, you will probably have noticed something else; the first 1/2in of core surface immediately adjacent to the two templates will be slightly higher than the rest of the cut surface (Fig. 4.5). This is quite normal, and is probably due to a slight amount of wire sag, possibly coupled with local cooling of the wire as it runs over the templates. It is to avoid this that professionals use stand-off templates. These two small humps can easily be eliminated by a little gentle sanding.

Whatever the first cut surface is like, you must go on and cut the other one. What you need is practice! If you are using single templates, leave them pinned to the block, replace the off-cut, turn the whole thing over, pile on the wood and weights, and you are ready for the second cut. If double templates are being used, unpin the upper ones, and replace them with the lower, without turning the block over. Replace the off-cut and weights. You can now make the second cut, in exactly the same way, but this time start from the leading edge. This point is very important, particularly if you are making cores for glider wings. Firstly, if you try to cut the upper surface from the leading edge back, you will be pushing the HWC, not in a horizontal direction, but at an angle of some 30-40 deg up over the sharply-climbing template edge

(Fig. 4.6). Even worse, if both cuts are made towards the trailing edge, the latter will emerge as a nasty, thick, melted mess, as experience has shown over and over again. If, however, you make the first cut from the trailing edge, and the second one towards it, you can produce the most incredibly sharp edge, which is exactly what you want for gliders.

Make the second cut, and you will have a complete foam core.

Before you throw it away, consider the following - it is quite possible to save an apparently bad core. If it is heavily granulated, there is not much point in trying, but if it is ridged, then keep it. Make up a large sanding board, which should be as long as the largest sheet of 400 grade emery paper that you can lay hands on, and about 2in wide. Place the core in one of the off-cuts, and then sand the surface all over. If you use short, circular strokes, working spanwise from one end to the other, you will see those ridges all disappear in short order. Do not use too much pressure, or the emery will dig in and tear the foam. If the emery paper begins a curious 'skating' motion, stop immediately and lift the board. One of the beads of foam - generally a particularly hard one - will have been torn out, and is now rolling between the sander and the surface. Blow all over the board and the foam to get rid of it (or them), otherwise you will dig grooves in the surface, which are very hard to eliminate.

Incidentally, this sanding process is most useful in its own right, because you will find that by doing it you will be able to use less glue when skinning, thus cutting down on the final weight.

Should there be one or two quite noticeable grooves in an otherwise acceptable wing they can, however, be satisfactorily filled. For many years I searched for a suitable filler for foam wings, my requirements were:

By cutting the second surface from leading edge to trailing edge, ultra-thin cores may be obtained.

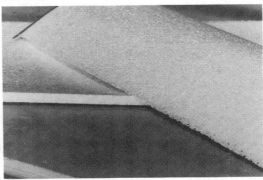

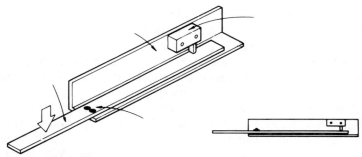

Fig. 4.7 Single-handed cutting foot-switch

(i) Chemically compatible, so polyester or solvent based fillers which attack foam were an obvious non-starter.(ii) Sanding properties similar to polystyrene for the final dressing.

(iii) Light-weight which eliminated Polyfilla.

Eventually I came up with a simple home brewed mix that I have used every since.

Simply take a small quantity of vinyl emulsion paint, add 10% water and mix to a stiff spreading consistency with micro-balloons. The resultant mix can then be easily spread onto the affected area, allowed to dry (it is air drying, so patience is needed) and finally sanded level.

Its sanding properties also make it suitable for balsa wood where it can be sanded without leaving a hard edge. It will accept either Copydex or epoxy wing adhesives without problem.

Another common fault when cutting close to the trailing edge is one end of the bow emerging before the other and falling off the template, leaving a pronounced gash on the TE close to the 'late' end. Simply cut out the damaged area and glue (PVA) a patch of foam into the area, sanding off when dry.

Single-handed cutting

To the newcomer reading this book prior to cutting his (or her) first pair of wings the prospect of cutting single-handed may appear daunting. This is not so if the process is approached sensibly. To the small commercial producer it is an economic necessity. The following methods are based on this aspect of wing cutting, but are equally suitable for home production.

The only extra piece of equipment needed is a foot-switch, which leaves both hands free to concentrate on the cutting

(Fig.4.7). The other major difference is that you will now stand facing the middle of the wing rather than at one end. Generally speaking the 'simple' bow is the preferred type on grounds of light weight and convenience. The blanks are prepared in the usual manner, presumably you have cut them solo anyway, which, in itself will have given you experience of handling the materials and tools.

The choice from the newcomer's point of view is whether to pull or push the cutter. Once you have made your choice and begun work you will probably remain with that direction. If you choose to work away from yourself (pushing), if other considerations make it desirable to cut one surface from the LE and one form the TE, the work can still be turned around. Counting around my acquaintances the choice would seem to be around two to one in favour of pushing rather like the on-going discussion on Mode 1 and Mode 2 transmitters - it depends on the instructor.

As with two-person cutting, it is obviously easier to begin with parallel chord wings.

Having set the blank up on the work top with the templates attached, place the bow on the templates right up against the work. The big advantage of the foot switch is that it allows everything to be correctly aligned 'cold'. A final check around to make sure that nothing has been left on the bench to impede the passage of the bow, check that you are not applying pressure to the bow. RELAX, and press the foot-switch. As the wire comes up to temperature begin to move the wire over the templates, letting the cutter find its own speed. A good indication of correct cutting speed is that the exposed ends of the wire are straight rather than swept back. During the cut, try to keep both ends traversing parallel, the ultimate aim being for both ends to emerge simultaneously. However, if 'pushing you will be unsighted, therefore keep moving until you have reached the extremes of the templates. Single or double templates may be used, but as usual, double templates will have the advantage.

By starting with parallel wings, preferably of a convenient size, say up to 30in half span you will soon gain confidence and will realise that is actually easier to be in total control. To further improve your skills, practise on any odd piece of foam, it does not have to produce a usable wing.

Cutting tapered wings solo is an acquired skill, but again can soon be mastered. Up to this stage the length of the bow has not

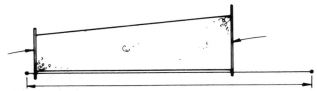

Fig. 4.8 Single-handed cutting start position

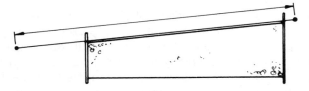

Fig. 4.9 Single-handed cutting finishing position

been critical, 2 - 3in over at each end is about normal, but a little longer is no great problem. For tapered wings it will be an advantage to select a bow some 1.3 to 1.4 times the length of the panel. Begin the cut with one leg of the bow close to the tip template (Fig.4.8) and move with a scything action, moving the bow sideways as well as forwards so that as the bow emerges the surplus wire will be at the tip (Fig.4.9). This does two things, firstly it continually introduces hot wire to the root end of the wing that needs to cut faster and conversely uses cooled wire from the centre of the core for cutting the tip. Secondly it gives the hand holding the bow at the tip of the wing further to travel, therefore, making it easier to move at a constant rate.

Good quality metal templates are invariably recommended for the tips of tapered panels, as the wire is moving slower and therefore has more time to burn notches in lesser materials. The speed of the cut is dictated by the rate over the root template which should not be forced above the natural speed of the wire. It is the tip which needs to be controlled, the knack is to be able to move at a constant rate with no obvious natural resistance to act as an indicator.

To perfect your technique make a few dry passes over dummy templates first, and then cut a few tailplanes - small panels are much easier. With practice root to tip ratios of 1.5:1 should ultimately be attainable.

The delta planform takes the differential between tip and root chords to the point where normal methods of cutting will not give consistent or satisfactory results. Examining the problem in

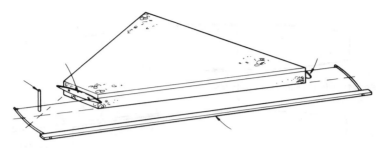

Fig. 4.10 Cutting delta cores

detail, it becomes apparent that if one could pivot the wire at the projected apex of the leading and trailing edges, a constant relative speed over both templates could be attained. First reactions are always 'that's easy - just tie one end to a nail and hold the other, 'cheese-cutter' style'. However, keeping sufficient or constant tension is far from easy. A more satisfactory system is to use a normal bow of sufficient length to give a slight overhang the other side of the nail. Mine is a length of 8 swg piano wire, plugged into the standard base board (Fig.4.10).

The cutting procedure is simple. Fix the templates (single or double) in the usual manner adjust the position of the core relative to the pillar apex, switch on the power. The wire at the root will cut at its normal speed, whilst the tip end of the bow will be restrained by the pillar. It will soon be found that an equal pressure can be maintained on both ends of the bow. There is even a bonus to be had with the system the pressure on the pillar will also take-up any slack in the wire. Cutting the other hand simply means moving the nail across the board.

Cutting delta core, the nail can be seen inthe lower right corner of the photograph. (Bill Burkenshaw photo)

Fig. 4.11 Effect of burn-out on delta core

Fig. 4.12 Modified template to counter burn-out

There is a well known 'law' dictating that such a simple solution is bound to have a down-side; this one has two, closely related to each other. Firstly, deltas bring about the most difficult scenario in terms of 'burn-out', this being the amount of foam burnt away by the slower moving wire at the tip. Whereas a normal wing may have a root/tip ratio of say 1.5:1., deltas may be 3 or 4 times this figure. The burn-out problem is further complicated by the fact that at the beginning of the cut the wire temperature is constant along its length, but as the cut progresses there is less and less cooling effect from the foam at the tip, leading to increased burn-out towards the trailing edge (Fig.4.11). The only way to counter this loss of foam is to anticipate it when actually making the template (Fig.4.12). Templates for delta tips should always be cut from metal, even the softer grades of aluminium will not stand up to continued use. Mild steel of 18-20 swg is favourite, which brings us neatly to draw-back number two. There will be local cooling at the actual template, leaving a raised edge to the finished core, which will require sanding off (refer back to Fig.4.5).

As deltas give a very visual indication of the problem this is a good time to consider another regrettably often overlooked aspect -storage of finished wings. It will be appreciated that the regular shaped block of foam that you started with is no longer totally flat, but is well down on one corner. This will also apply to any tapered wing although it may be less obvious. Consider now the effect on the bottom wings if they are stacked up six or seven pairs high! Distortion of your carefully cut wings will occur. Of course not everyone will have that many wings - but even one pair stored flat with anything heavy on top will warp. The answer

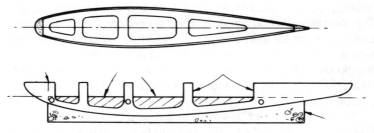

Fig. 4.13 Cutting hollow cores

is to store wings on the leading edges, or even vertical on the roots. Storage conditions should be cool and dry, avoid the roof space at all costs. The temperature variations can play havoc with unsealed foam wings.

Light-weight hollow wings

Certain applications call for wings to be as light as possible, whilst still enjoying the advantages of foam construction. The two most popular types in this quest are control line 'stunt' and R/C 'Fun-Fly'. They also have other common factors and resistance to span-wise bending moment is not a prime requirement. This presents a good case for removing unwanted material from the middle of the core.

The most satisfactory way of achieving this is to cut each panel in two parts split top and bottom, removing the lightening section before joining and skinning (Fig.4.13).

If, by good fortune (or design) your wing is symmetrical in section you will only need one set of templates for each end.

Fully symmetrical wings

Fully symmetrical wings, beloved of competition aerobatic designers and fliers, depend on the accuracy of the template

Hollow core with hole cut for GRP joining tube. (Sid King photo)

making, for an exact match between top and bottom surfaces. This problem can be circumvented by only making one side and turning it over for the second cut. A further advantage is that the rear line can be extended beyond the actual trailing edge allowing an overlap cut, as used in normal double template cutting, thus eliminating the need for substantial wooden trailing edge or aileron material.

The practicalities of this system are slightly more complex than first impressions suggest. But they are nevertheless easy to follow.

Having established the centre line and attached the (half) template in the usual way, cut the first surface as normal, carefully remove the nails, reverse the template relocating the nail in the original holes. It is at this point that the weakness in the system shows up.

Although accurately located, the templates will not be as firmly attached. There are, however, two possible corrective choices, one is simply to use longer nails (of the same diameter of course) or to use extra nails in two auxiliary holes. Either way, this is a method that will produce very accurate competition wings.

Elliptical wings

As a hot-wire cutter can only cut in straight lines, the production of truly elliptical wings (e.g. 'Spitfire') is not possible. At least, such was popular belief until the mid 1980s when an ingenious modeller (I believe in Czechoslovakia) realised that, by taking a common fault and exaggerating it, elliptical wings can indeed be cut. The fault in point is that of trailing edge thickness variation caused by the cutting board being bent. In short if it is not possible to bend the cutting wire, then bend the foam block in the opposite direction (Fig.4.15).

After cutting, the block will resume its original shape but the cut will be curved (Fig.4.16).

This technique can be exploited in many ways. The simplest of which will give an elliptical wing core but will leave the leading and trailing edges straight to be filled out later. Production of this wing commences with a perfectly normal tapered wing blank with the root and tip templates attached, incorporating any washout required.

To establish the amount of bend required you will need to refer to the front view of the wing (Fig.4.17) plotting straight lines from the template positions (Lines A - A). This will establish two vital dimensions - the amount of bend i.e. the distances A and B (they

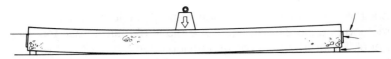

Fig. 4.15 The basic principle of achieving a curved cut

Fig. 4.16 The resultant curved cut

Fig. 4.17 Establishing the offset required for curved cut

will not be the same unless it is a symmetrical section) and the point of maximum curvature (X-X). If a front view of the wing is not available, then a section plotted at point X-X will yield the same information.

Returning to the workpiece, it is advantageous to cut the bottom surface first. This surface will usually have less curvature and will therefore require less weight to bend the blank (once the first cut is completed, the blank will bend more easily). Place the blank upside down on the board, pack each end up to the dimension B required for the bottom surface, place sufficient weight at point X to bend the foam down to the board and cut as normal.

To cut the top surface turn the blank over, substitute the end packing to suit dimension A for the top of the wing, replace the weights and make the second cut. You will now have the basis of an elliptical wing, although it will still need shaping in the plan view. This can be achieved in two ways. Either skin the wing as normal and add relatively wide balsa leading and trailing edges to build up the required shape. This method is best suited to smaller models. The alternative is to boost the shape with foam off-cuts, carving and finally sanding to shape before skinning.

This elliptical cutting technique is not necessarily limited to 'Spitfire' wings but can equally well be employed for wings having elliptical tips only, by simply moving the weights out to the appropriate position and packing up the tip template only.

Saw-cutting blue foam cores

So far we have investigated methods of cutting cores with a HWC. There is, however, a way of making cores with a small saw but it will really only work on blue foam. White foam would rip. The method is quite simple. Cut out a block of foam to suit the wing panel. Either free-hand or with a single template, draw the aerofoil on the ends of the block with a felt-tipped pen. Next, draw tangents to this aerofoil. Where the ends of the tangents intersect the top and bottom surfaces, pin small strips of hardwood in place, in such a way that the saw-blade, when laid across them, will follow the lines. Finally, saw along the panel, and you will end up with a block of foam which is cut to an angular approximation of the aerofoil section required.

To obtain the true section, you will now need to use a long sanding block and a fair bit of elbow-grease. This will require some 'eyeballing', but is not difficult to do - however, do remember that it is far easier to remove foam than to replace it!

Wing-tips

Since we are on the subject, let us discuss making wing-tips in general. Here, we are no longer talking about scale models, but sports planes. The simplest possible tip is a plain balsa block, which is stuck to the end of the wing panel, after skinning, and then cut and sanded down until it fairs in to the lines of the panel. When doing this, take care not to cut into the veneer. Protect it with a strip of sticky tape. If weight is a problem, the block can be hollowed out, or even built-up, bread-and-butter fashion, which is also a good way of using up scraps of balsa.

A second kind of wing-tip, also very simple to make, is the 45 deg type. In this case, set up two 45 deg set-squares on the edge of the work-surface, place the core so that it just overhangs the edge of the surface, between the two set-squares, and then slice off the extreme tip of the panel with the HWC. The core is then skinned in the usual way, and the skins sanded flush with

Cutting a core from blue foam, using wood strips and a small saw. Finish the job by sanding.

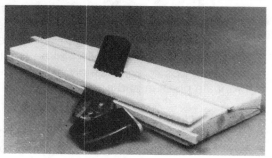

this 45 deg edge. Finally, a piece of veneer is stuck to the tip and sanded flush.

There are, of course, other ways of making tips, but most of them are variations of those already described. You will no doubt discover others as your modelling in foam progresses.

Computer controlled cutting

By far the most significant development in recent years is the harnessing of computer capability to control the hot wire. At the time of writing, cost alone would limit this to commercial enterprise - a basic cost of around ú6,000 for the cutting equipment alone, assuming a suitable computer is available. Not then for the home hobbyist, but no book on foam cutting would be complete without acknowledging this major advance.

The equipment consists of a flat bed long enough to accommodate the longest wing panel required. Each end unit comprises of a ceramic eye through which the hot wire passes. The posi-

The balsa tip block is cut roughly to shape, stuck in place with epoxy glue, and held with sticky tape.

The finished tip, nicely sanded to blend into the contour of the wing.

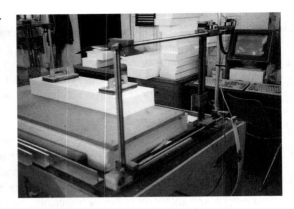

Computerised cutter in action. (Sid King photo - courtesy of Flair Products)

tion of the eye is controlled by two geared electric motors, one moving it in the vertical axis, whilst the other governs movement in the horizontal direction. The relative positions of the two opposing eyes are therefore infinitely variable. The end units can also be adjusted span-wise to suit shorter workpieces. As the wire position is accurately controlled by the motor units, no templates are necessary, instead the software programmes the relative positions of each 'eye' in sequence to give the required section such is the level of sophistication that the programme supplied contains a whole selection of known 'standard' sections (e.g. Eppler 193, RG15 etc) which can be called up at will from the menu. The chord dimension at either end can be specified or individual requirements for wing sections can be programmed in using the numerical ordinates. The traverse speed (cm/min) is also variable.

The advantages are that given consistency in the raw material, accuracy is guaranteed and that once loaded and set in motion the machine will happily whirl away leaving the operative free to carry out another short-term task.

5 WING SKINNING

Skins and adhesives

It must be said, straight from the beginning, that this is a very extensive subject, and a whole book could be devoted to it. We will take a look at the most common methods.

Having cut your cores, you will have noticed that they are very floppy, and that it is obvious that strength has to be added before they can possibly be used in a model. Covering them with a skin, and, perhaps, adding reinforcement is the answer. Let's take a look at skins. Probably the most popular is obechi, which is a veneer of fairly light tropical wood. The DIY store is no good this time. You will have to contact one of the specialists who advertise in the model press. Most commercially-manufactured kits with foam wings have obechi skins.

The second choice is balsa - it is certainly used a great deal on the Continent and in the USA. A skin which seems to be gaining in popularity is ordinary brown wrapping paper, perhaps because of its low cost. Another up-and-coming method is not to use a true skin, but to reinforce blue foam panels with balsa spars, and then to iron-on film directly onto the foam. After this we enter the field of GRP and composite skins, which, although rarer, certainly have their place in competition and scale models.

The choice of adhesive is wide, but it is possible to categorise the different types. The most popular, because of the rapidity they bring to the skinning process, are contact glues, such as Copydex. Copydex has become the generic term for latex/ammonia based adhesives. Regrettably, it is rarely seen in quantities of more than a few ounces, which is usually uneconomic for the quantities we need. Try the large DIY superstores where 1.5 or even 2.5 litres are sometimes available. However, a better source will be your local friendly carpet-fitter, who will call it 'latex adhesive' and rarely travels without a couple of 5 litre cans.

Various types of contact adhesives used for skinning wings. The disply Mount and Photo Mount are in aerosol cans.

A word of warning here. Never use neoprene-based contact glue, because it will eat foam at a voracious rate. When in doubt, always check for glue reaction on a piece of scrap foam.

White glue is a popular choice but it takes longer to grip the skin, so the process is much more time-consuming. However, as we shall see, there is a way of using white glue which is almost as rapid as contact glue. The third possibility is to use epoxy glues or resins, which is my favourite, even if there is some degree of overkill in their use on the smaller models. On the larger models there is a definite advantage, since they make wing reinforcing very easy to achieve.

In this chapter, and the next, we shall take a look at a variety of methods, some of which may require some slight modifications to the foam core, which must be taken into account when the cores are being cut.

Going back to our 50in Clark Y wing, we must decide whether or not it will feature ailerons. We will start by considering a non-aileron wing, skinned with obechi and contact glue, and with a separate LE spar. The trailing edge will be formed by the glued edge between the upper and lower surface skins (Fig. 5.1).

Applying the skin

Once the cores have been finely sanded and brushed off, use them as patterns for marking out and cutting up the two upper surface and two lower surface skins from the sheet of obechi. Use a very sharp modelling knife, taking care not to split the veneer. The skins should be slightly larger all round than the cores; don't forget to allow for the curvature of the core section, particularly on the upper surface.

The Copydex is dry, and the core placed in its off-cut, covered with a sheet of fairly thick polythene except for about an inch at the the leading edge.

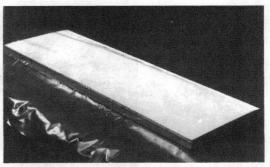

Once place on the core, the skin is glued at the leading edge, and can now be smoothed down on the core.

Spread a thin coating of Copydex on the lower surface of one core and the relevant obechi skin. Because of the glue's lack of colour this is not easy, since you will find it difficult to see those areas where there is hardly any glue, and those where it is too thick. To avoid this problem, put a few drops of kitchen colouring, such as cochineal, into the glue, and mix well. This makes it much easier to check on glue density. The whole point is that you should use only enough glue to ensure that the two surfaces stick well together, and no more, otherwise you are adding weight to the panel - weight that your model can well do without if it is to fly correctly.

Put the core in its off-cut, glued side uppermost, take the skin and hold it accurately in place just above the core. A good tip is to place a piece of polyethylene sheet, such as is used for gardening purposes, between the core and the wing. Position the core, and then carefully pull out the plastic sheet. Do not use Clingfilm for this job; it does not work! Make sure that the skin is properly glued to the core by rubbing it with a piece of rag and quite a lot of pressure. When you are satisfied, remove the core from the off-cut, and trim the LE, root and tip, with a sharp modelling knife. The TE

The skin is finally glued down in place on the core.

The balsa leading edge spar is glued in place and held firmly with sticky tape.

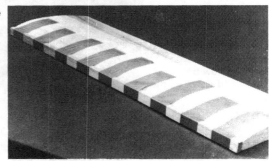

A cross-section of the skinned wing - the leading edge hs been sanded to shape.

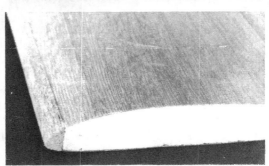

should be sanded very carefully, until it blends with the shape of the upper surface - this will give a good glue joint. Repeat for the upper surface. Make sure that the off-cut is resting on a perfectly flat surface, otherwise there will be a twist in the wing, which will do the flying performance no good at all. Check that the two skins are stuck accurately and properly at the TE.

Remove the panel from its off-cut, trim all round with a sharp knife, and then glue the LE spar in place. Here a slow-setting epoxy is preferable. However, if weight is critical, bear in mind that there is a basic difference between epoxies and regular

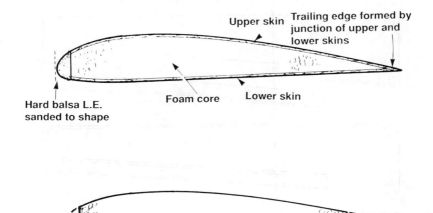

Upper skin — Trailing edge formed by junction of upper and lower skins

Hard balsa L.E. sanded to shape

Foam core   Lower skin

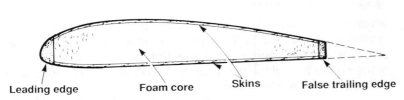

Foam core

Leading edge   Foam core   Skins   False trailing edge

Fig. 5.4 False trailing edge spar

wood working adhesives (e.g. PVA 'white-glue' and aliphatic) - epoxies 'cure' once the two components are mixed, they do not loose any of their weight, whereas wood working glues 'dry' and in doing so shed a proportion of the applied weight.

Use clear adhesive tape to hold the spar in place whilst the glue is drying. All that then remains is to plane and sand the LE down to the desired shape in the usual way. The second panel is made just like the first (Fig. 5.2).

Adding ailerons

If the wing is to be fitted with ailerons, a slightly different approach is required. The template can be used as before, but one solution is to reduce the width of the foam block by the width of the ailerons that are to be fitted, plus that of a false TE spar,

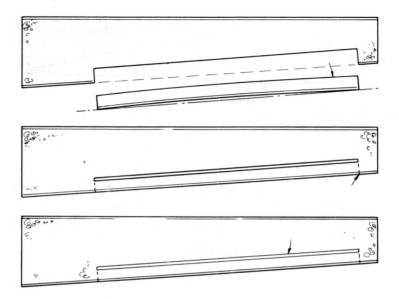

Fig. 5.5 Cutting ailerons from cores

which will be used both to reinforce the panel and also for hinging the aileron (Fig. 5.3). The latter can be made of trailing edge stock, or a planed and sanded sheet of balsa. The trailing edge of the centre part of the wing can be made in the same way, and then stuck to the false TE spar.

Alternatively, you can make the wing with a foam core skinned right back to the TE, and then cut out the ailerons with a very sharp knife. In this case it will be necessary not only to add a false TE spar to the wing panel, but also to face the cut edge of the aileron with sheet wood, the thickness of which will depend on the hinging method chosen (Fig. 5.4). For gliders and small planes you can use iron-on film or Scotch Magic Tape, but for the larger power models, proper hinges are a better choice, so the wood must be thick enough to afford sufficient strength to pin them in place.

When cutting ailerons out of a wing, particularly if the wing is very thin, there is often a tendency for the ailerons to bow outwards (Fig.5.5A). High aspect ratio glider wings and pylon racer wings are frequently affected in this way. To counter this, remove a slot in the wing, equal to the combined widths of the false trailing edge and the aileron leading edge, spot-tack these two com-

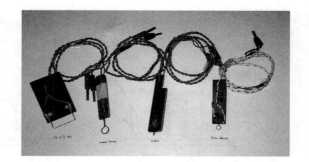

ponents together and glue them into the slot. When dry, careful-ly cut out the ends of the aileron.

The foregoing presumes the use of strip ailerons, in which case some sort of torque rod mechanism will be used. This will create no installation problems. Inset ailerons can be actuated by torque rods, but snakes or bellcranks are the usual method. Here some extra work must be done on the core before skinning.

In both cases, it will be necessary to make a channel, usually in the underside of the core, through which the snake outer or the bellcrank pushrod can run (Fig. 5.5). This may be done with a modelling knife, but there are two better ways. One is to use the tip of a soldering iron, with a metal ruler laid on the surface to keep the run straight. The second is to build a special HWC, a miniature one, which is made mostly from scrap, will only cost a few pence, and which is extremely useful. It can be used not only

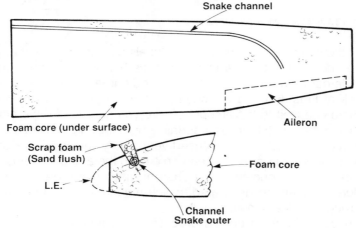

Snake channel

Foam core (under surface)

Aileron

Scrap foam
(Sand flush)

Foam core

L.E.

Channel
Snake outer

Fig. 5.6 Control runs in foam core

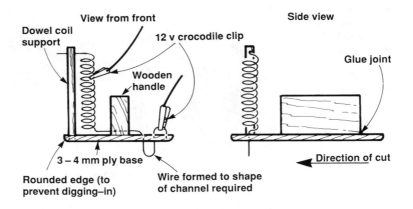

View from front

Dowel coil
support

12 v crocodile clip

Wooden
handle

Side view

Glue joint

3 – 4 mm ply base

Rounded edge (to
prevent digging–in)

Wire formed to shape
of channel required

Direction of cut

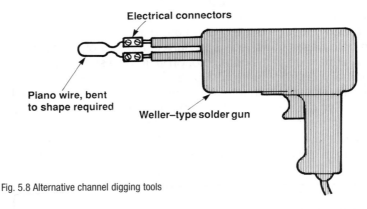

Electrical connectors

Piano wire, bent
to shape required

Weller–type solder gun

Fig. 5.8 Alternative channel digging tools

for the snake and pushrod runs, but also for other holes that you may need to cut in the foam, such as holes for the bellcranks, undercarriage blocks, retracting undercarriages, and so on. A look at Figs. 5.6 and 5.7 should tell you all you need to know. There is a limit to the amount of wire you can use for the actual cutting, because beyond a certain length the wire will not be stiff enough. This tool must be used very slowly, letting it work at its own speed. Be careful to keep an eye on the ammeter if you use a thicker wire, because your charger may quickly be at its limit. More heat will be generated, which means that the tool will go through the foam more rapidly.

A good tip when cutting grooves for cable outers is to cut a template of the route required with a definite relationship to the

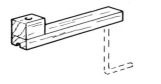

Fig. 5.9 Traditional block undercarriage mounting

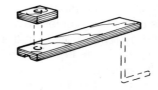

Fig. 5.10 Recommended modified undercarriage mounting

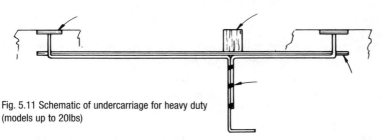

Fig. 5.11 Schematic of undercarriage for heavy duty (models up to 20lbs)

trailing edge and wing root an off-cut of veneer is a suitable material. Having established that the chosen cable-run does not interfere with any other installations such as undercarriages or flat servos, run the cutting tool around the template. Do not discard the template, as it will then indicate the position and exit point of the cable after the wing is skinned.

In fact, there is a third way of making these channels, and that is to use a small electric router; but be warned, choose your workplace very carefully! A router will throw tiny bits of foam out all over the place, and because it sticks to everything by static electrical charges, it really is most awkward to get rid of.

There is often differing opinion about when best to cut these holes, but to my mind it is a much easier task before the foam is skinned. The snake or pushrod outers are glued into their channels with epoxy or white PVA glue, the channel filled in, if necessary, with scrap foam, allowed to dry before skinning, and then sanded carefully flush with the surface of the wing panel. Servo and undercarriage block holes are cut out, the wing skinned, and the skin then cut to reveal the holes.

Obviously, some designs will call for a wing-mounted undercarriage. This is the area where most damage to a wing is likely to occur. The traditional method is to use the same grooved beech blocks that were used before foam wings came along (Fig.5.9). Regrettably they are only supported on the bottom surface of the wing (unless a sub-rib is inserted) the net result being that they tend to pivot on the back edge of the block and move inside the foam. Foam, as a basic material has little 'memory', it can't remember what shape it was before it hit the ground, so makes little effort to return to it.

A more recent development has been to use a lighter but broader main bearer from grooved 25 x 6mm ply supporting the top of the undercarriage wire in a piece of 6mm ply 25 x 25mm inserted into the top of the wing, usually in the area reinforced by the joining bandage (Fig.5.10).

For larger models this system can be extended to utilise two torsion bars, one running inboard from the leg and another extending outwards (Fig.5.11). By making them two different lengths a degree of damping is also achieved. I have used this set-up in a model of 11 kilos with 6swg legs, but would consider 9 kilos as a safe maximum.

When someone mentions 'retracts' in a foam wing I usually emit a low groan, followed by a very restrained 'if you must'. Yes, it can be done, but to my mind it is not satisfactory. Depending on the size of model and type of unit, sufficient timber work can be installed in the foam, but it may be easier to make a build-up central section and add foam outer panels.

The best solution, particularly on larger models, is to construct a ply box, the full depth of the wing, to house all the retract components and incorporate this into the wing-joining method.

By making the box full depth it will then be in contact with the fuselage, thus transmitting much of the shock direct between the heavy bits and the wheels.

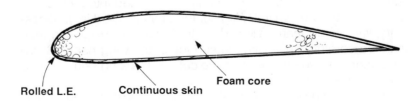

Rolled L.E. **Continuous skin** **Foam core**

Fig. 5.12 Rolled leading edge skin

Rolling veneer

As has been mentioned already, there is another way of skinning a wing. By rolling the veneer around the leading edge there is no need for a LE spar (Fig. 5.12). You will need a foam core which is complete, and not with the LE portion cut off, as was the previous case. Once again, contact glue is used, but this time, instead of cutting two skin panels for each wing panel, a single one is used, large enough to cover upper and lower surfaces. The danger with this method is that if the LE of the foam core has a fairly small radius, the wood skin will split as it is forced round it. To avoid this, there are two things you can do. One is to wet the outside of the skin. The second is to obtain some parcel tape about 3in wide and stick it on the outside of the skin where it will be wrapped round the front edge of the foam core. Rub it quite heavily to make sure it has a good purchase on the wood. This will help avoid splitting.

Next coat the inside of the skin and the core with contact glue, as before. Now comes the tricky bit. The core must be carefully lowered into place on the skin. If anything goes wrong at this stage, you have got problems, because contact glue is a one-shot affair. Either you get it right first time or you throw it away and start again! Once it is safely in place, you have to slide one hand under the core, steadying it with the other, and then slowly roll the LE of the core onto the skin, keeping enough pressure on it to ensure that the two surfaces are gradually glued together (Fig. 5.13). This is much easier to do than to explain. Work slowly,

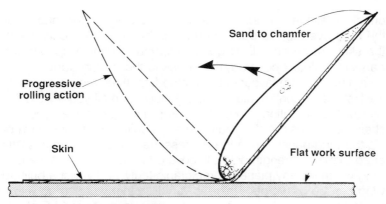

Fig. 5.13 Stages in rolling leading edge

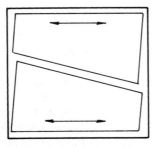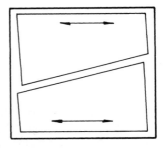

Fig. 5.14 Veneer grain directions for tapered wing

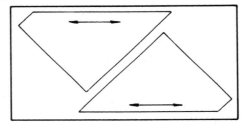

Fig. 5.15 Veneer grain directions for delta

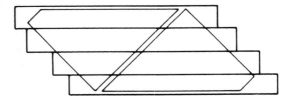

Fig. 5.16 Balsa sheet layout for delta planform

checking all the time that the skin is glued evenly. Continue to roll the core over so the upper surface is brought into contact with the skin. In the end, if all goes well, you will finish up with the panel completely covered, right back to the trailing edge.

I am not really in favour of this method, for three main reasons. In the first place, contact glue is instantaneous, and if you get the first part of the operation wrong, there is practically no way you can straighten things out. Secondly, there is a quite definite risk of warping the wing panel during the process, because the foam has little or no torsional strength until it is covered on both sides. A warped wing will make any plane unpredictable to fly, and whilst a built-up wing can be un-warped, there is very little that you can do with a twisted foam-cored wing. Thirdly, repairing a damaged LE of this kind is more difficult. Nevertheless, wings of this type are popular, so if you want to have a go at one, don't be put off If you intend to incorporate ailerons, build them in exactly the same way as for the spar LE wing.

Balsa wood does not come cheap so the following method will save a fair slice of your outlay, if you are making tapered or delta wings, although not quite so critical. The principle also applies to obechi veneer.

By reversing the two tapered panels against each other (Fig.5.14) a rectangle will be formed, obviously using less material than two rectangles to the span x root chord dimension. Nothing too compli- cated here, but to watch out for the hidden trap - both the skins from one rectangle will be the same 'hand'. Therefore the normal routine is to take the top of one wing from the first rectangle and the bottom skin of the same wing from the second rectangle.

It is usually more convenient to apply the adhesive to the com- plete rectangle even when using veneer empoying this routine you will avoid perhaps the greatest mistake of all - 'crossed grains'. This is when the veneer is applied to a tapered wing with the grain parallel to the leading edge on one surface and paral- lel to the trailing edge on the opposing side. This gives the effect of up to 30 deg crossover in plan view - a warped wing in a few days is almost guaranteed.

Returning to delta plan forms, the problems are exaggerated by the large dead areas beyond the trailing edges (Fig.5.15). The unusable areas can be reduced by staggering the balsa-sheets

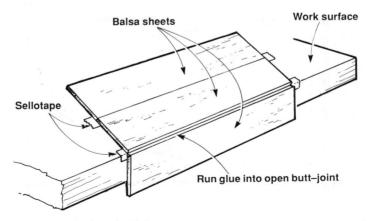

Fig. 5.17 Assembling skins from sheet balsa

when making up the skins, consequently using less material - do a trial lay-out first (Fig.5.16).

Other materials

The two methods described have both used obechi skinning, which is the most popular material, but it is not the only one. Balsa is just as effective. We have mentioned its popularity on the Continent, and undoubtedly it gives a much better finish when used with an iron-on film finish. The only difference when using balsa is that you will have to join several sheets - for the wing in question I would suggest 2mm or 3/32in to make up skins of sufficient width. This is most easily done by laying the planks on your work-surface, edge to edge, and then temporarily joining them lengthwise with a strip of clear adhesive tape. Turn them over and open up each joint, into which you can then run a very thin fillet of white glue (Fig. 5.17). Replace the sheets on the work surface, so that the joint is closed again, and give it a wipe with a damp sponge, to get rid of the excess glue which has been squeezed out. When dry, the skin can be used to cover the core in the same way as before.

Another material, used where great strength is required, or where you need to respect the chosen aerofoil as closely as possible, is 1/64in plywood, but this is better left until you have some experience at the job - and when you really need it. I have even seen F3B contest glider wings with a foam core and a Formica

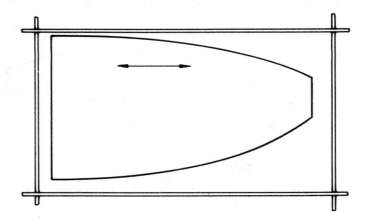

Fig. 5.18 Veneer for eliptical wing

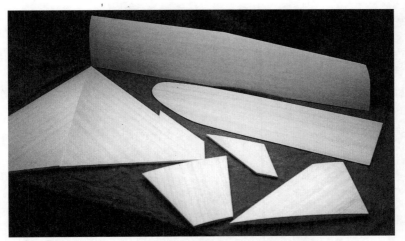

A selection of foam wing panels ready for despatch. Examples include elliptical tips, delta and tapered panels

skin, but whilst the finish is impeccable and the strength high, they seem prone to shattering on impact. Leave them to those who really need them, though, in fact, the skinning technique is the same.

Skinning elliptical wings

As with cutting, elliptical wing skinning is a special case; in fact the amount of double curvature possible on a wing is often limited not by the cutting operation but by the skinning. The average 'Spitfire' wing is just about on the limit. For contact adhesive, the technique is to prepare the skins comparatively oversized, apply the contact adhesive and allow to dry. Place the core in its off-cut on a flat surface which has been marked out with sight-lines, in coloured adhesive tape (Fig.5.18). Using the sight-lines as a guide, gently lower the skin onto the highest point, make firm contact by pressing gently on the high point, then work out from the centre in stages, avoiding kinking the skin, trim-off and repeat for the other surface.

6 FURTHER SKINNING TECHNIQUES

Reinforcement

In the previous chapter we looked at methods of skinning wings using contact glue, but this is not the only adhesive available to us, even if it is the quickest-acting. It is perfectly possible to use white glue (PVA), and if it is used correctly, results can be nearly as quick as contact glue, even if a little preparation is required. The entire wing is not skinned, only the part as far back as the maximum thickness point of the chord. False cap strips are then used further aft to the trailing edge. The result is that the wing looks very much like a built-up wing - providing you don't use transparent film, of course - which means that it can be used for scale and semi-scale models (Fig. 6.1).

Since we do not use complete skins, it is necessary to reinforce the wing spanwise.

Probably the easiest way of reinforcing a wing is to use a full-depth ply spar. On a 72in. span glider wing, for example, a spar of 2mm good quality plywood is quite sufficient. In order to fit such a spar, it is necessary to cut the core in half spanwise at the appropriate place. This is easily done by placing the core between the two set-squares used for sizing-up the original foam block, chocking it up, if necessary, to get the cut at right-angles to the chord line, then slicing it in two with the HWC. Theoretically, it is then necessary to make a second cut to remove the equivalent thickness of the spar, but in reality, the added thickness of a 2mm spar is going to make no difference at all to the performance of the wing, so it is hardly worth the trouble (Fig. 6.2).

To re-assemble the core, cover the lower off-cut with a layer of Clingfilm, purloined from the kitchen. This is necessary to prevent the core being glued to the off-cut. Coat the two faces of the spar with a thin coating of PVA glue and sandwich it between the two core halves, on the off-cut, leaving them to dry thoroughly. Weights or sticky tape will hold everything in place. Repeat for the other panel.

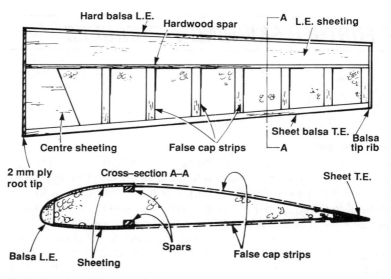

Fig. 6.1 Plan view of false cap-strip wing panel

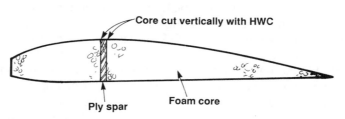

Fig. 6.2 Full-depth ply wing spar

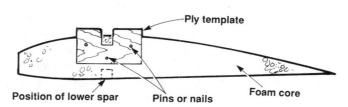

Fig. 6.3 Spruce spar templates

On small wings, up to 72in span, it is perfectly possible to use a one-piece spar, thus making a unitary wing. Whilst this may cause a few problems in transporting the wing to the flying field, structurally it is quite a good solution, because it avoids having to find another method of joining the two halves, a subject we will deal with later.

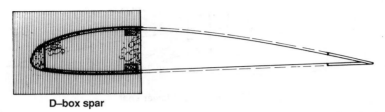

D–box spar

Fig. 6.4 D-box spar

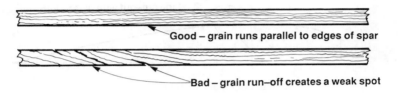

Good – grain runs parallel to edges of spar

Bad – grain run–off creates a weak spot

Fig. 6.5 Grain direction in spruce spars

An alternative is to make up two small templates, as shown in Fig. 6.3, pinning them onto the core in the appropriate place, and then cutting channels on both sides of the wing to take spruce spars. These spars, together with the LE sheeting, will form a very strong D-box spar (Fig. 6.4). The choice of spar material is up to you - my preference is for 10 x 3mm spruce. Whatever you use, there is an important rule to be respected; when you buy the spars, check the grain, which must run from one end of the spar to the other and not run out part way along. If you choose anything but good, straight-grained wood, you will be risking breakage (Fig. 6.5). Avoid wood with knots. Don't forget to check the grain, not only on what will eventually be the horizontal surface of the spar, but also on the sides. If you are building a very long wing panel, it is as well to reinforce the spar by laying a strip of glass-fibre tape of appropriate width on the inner surface of the spar, attaching it solidly with cyanoacrylate glue or epoxy. This will make the panel a great deal stronger. The spar is finally fixed in its channel in the foam with PVA or epoxy glue.

There is yet another, very efficient way of reinforcing a foam panel. In this case you need another pair of templates (Fig. 6.6). A semi-circular channel is cut in the surface of the foam core, and the off-cut is carefully put to one side. A length of thin glass cloth (2oz maximum) is fitted in the channel. This is then wetted

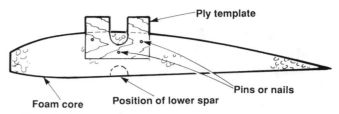

Ply template

Foam core   Position of lower spar   Pins or nails

Fig. 6.6 Glass-cloth and resin spar template

3. Replace foam off–cut and weight

2. Line cut–out with glass cloth and resin

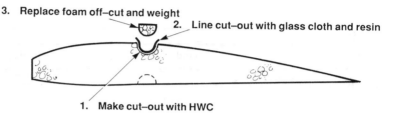

1. Make cut–out with HWC

4. Sand protruding material flush when resin has set

Fig. 6.7 Construction of GRP spars

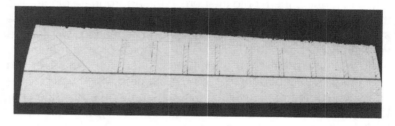

A core destined to bear false ribs and part sheeting, has been marked with a felt pen to show where it has to be painted wiht white glue.

with epoxy resin, the off-cut put back in place on top of it, and weights placed along the whole, to force the off-cut as far back into its original position as possible. When it is dry, the operation is repeated on the other side of the wing. It is best to carry out this work with the core lying in its own off-cuts, to ensure that no warping takes place. Lastly, cut and sand the raised edges carefully back to the surface of the core.

This method provides strong and very light reinforcement (Fig. 6.7).

We can now assume that you have your foam cores reinforced, ready for balsa skinning. You will need a supply of 2mm balsa of as light a grade as possible, some PVA glue with a colorant in it

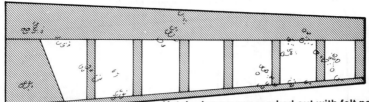

Hatched areas are marked out with felt pen and then brushed with diluted and coloured White glue on both sides of panel

Fig. 6.8 Marking-out foam core for false cap strips

A small travelling iron is used over the sheeting to reactivate the white glue. A small piece of balsa should be used to protect the foam from the heat of the iron.

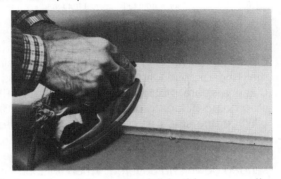

- white glue on white foam is not the most visible thing around! - and a wide brush to spread the glue. The first job is to mark out the core. Obviously there is no point in putting glue on places where there will be no skin; it only adds needless weight. With a very light-coloured felt pen, mark out the core as shown in Fig. 6.8. Spread a coat of PVA (thinned if necessary with water) on skin and core, and leave it to dry thoroughly. Don't worry if the balsa tends to curl up slightly; this will be taken care of in the actual skinning process.

To carry out the skinning, you will need an iron. An ordinary household iron is better for this job than the specialised ones designed for film covering. Place the core in its lower off-cut, put the upper surface LE sheeting in place, hold it firmly, and go over the whole sheet with the hot iron. As you do so, the heat will penetrate the wood and re-activate the glue. The effect is similar to using contact glue, but you have more chance to position your skinning accurately. Trial and error is the only way to judge the correct iron setting - if it burns the wood, it is too hot; but if the glue does not take, it is not hot enough! You will have to experiment.

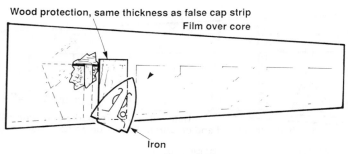

Fig. 6.9 Protection of foam from radiated heat from iron

Once the LE is done, tackle the TE sheeting, and finally the false cap strips. A certain amount of care is needed here because you will find that the heat from the iron may well start to melt the exposed foam between the strips. The remedy is to place a spare piece of balsa without any PVA on it beside the strip being glued, to protect the foam (Fig. 6.9).

When one side has been skinned, the core is turned over and laid in the other off-cut, and the process repeated. The balsa leading edge is added, and then the whole panel can then be sanded down and covered. When finished it will be difficult to tell the difference between this and a built-up wing. In addition, there is a worthwhile saving in materials, and thus weight.

GRP-reinforced obechi skins

The next method is used almost exclusively for the manufacture of large glider wings - that is, in excess of 110in span. Indeed, the sort of thing the average modeller dreams about, but which he thinks is well beyond his financial and technical capabilities. I used to! But these wings are just as easy to build as the others, and there is considerable pride in owning a 3.5m or 4m scale sailplane which one has built oneself, instead of from a kit.

The materials used are white or blue foam, balsa or obechi veneer, some glass cloth and epoxy resin. Don't be put off by the mention of resin, as so many modellers seem to be. There is a certain mystique surrounding the use of this seemingly exotic material which is quite unjustified, because it is as easy to use as epoxy glue. In addition, modern epoxies are now sold with full instructions for use, and even a child could handle them easily. Respect these instructions, work in a well-ventilated place, and don't rush - the pot-life (the time the resin will take to polymerise, or set) is more than long enough for you to take your time and get things right. Setting time is much greater than polyester resin, which must not be used in this context because it will attack the foam.

The advantages of epoxy are many. You can make a wing which is immensely strong but relatively light. It will not warp with time; and you can use some of the latest and most efficient aerofoils, which can lead to constructional difficulties with a built-up wing. About the only disadvantage is that building time is a little longer, because of the need to let the resin set. I have made wings using all the other methods described, but I have gradually chosen to build almost exclusively with epoxy resin, even for quite small wings.

Of course, our HWC is only capable of cutting panels of about 39in, and foam, particularly the blue variety, is often available only in limited lengths. The simple answer is to cut each panel in two sections. This is a slight complication, because we shall need a third template, but it is also an advantage, because it means that if we wish, we can construct a wing with a section that changes towards the tip to avoid tip stalling, a problem that is prevalent with the narrow tip chords found on very high aspect ratio wings. Aerodynamics are not within the scope of this book, but a typical example would be a 4m sailplane with Eppler 203 at the root, progressing to Eppler 201 at mid-span, and Eppler 193 at the tip. This will give a wing which is less prone to tip-stalling, despite the fact that it uses no washout, which in any case can have a detrimental effect on performance.

The first job is to draw up and cut out the templates. I would strongly advise the use of double, or split, templates. You will see why in a moment. Decide the length of the two sections - normally half-span, though this will depend on the planform of the wing; there may be a place where the taper changes, for instance, and

Foam core No. 1

Foam core No. 2

The join in the two panels is not necessarily at the mid–panel point

Fig. 6.10 Planform of double taper wing panel

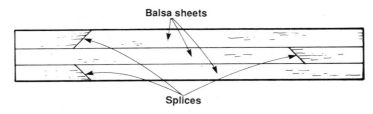

Balsa sheets

Splices

Fig. 6.11 Making up long balsa skins

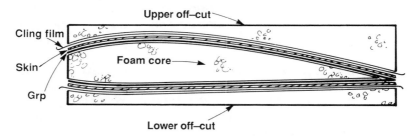

Upper off–cut

Cling film

Skin

Foam core

Grp

Lower off–cut

Fig. 6.12 Cross section of skinning sandwich (root)

the join will obviously be made here (Fig. 6.10). The root and tip templates are used in the normal way, but the second, or intermediary template, is used twice, as the tip plate for the inner section and the root plate for the outer. If you cut an extra template for the root of the outer panel you will find it much more difficult to get a smooth transition between the two sections.

A little planning needs to be done, because when the cores have been cut, it will be necessary not only to glue the two sections together, but also the off-cuts, so that they can be used in the skinning process. In other words, you have to work out the height of the chord lines of the three templates in such a way that when the complete core is laid in the glued-together off-cuts, it is perfectly flat. If this is not so, you will inevitably end up with a bent wing! A little common sense and calculation will show you that the task is not difficult. You can now see why I advocate the use of split templates - if you rely on the single type, and the template moves slightly during the cutting, you will have a terrible time trying to match-up the ends of the two sections, because they will either be at different heights, or one may be slightly twisted with respect to the other, resulting in a warped wing.

Having worked this out, cut each section as already described. Unless the aerofoil is very thin, white foam is quite adequate.

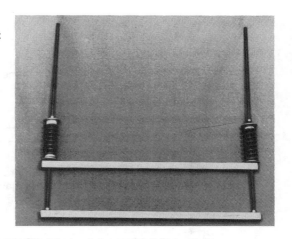
The spring press - a simple accessory, but very useful.

Place the two lower off-cuts of one wing panel end to end, line them up with a straight edge if necessary, and glue them together with a little five-minute epoxy. Cover them with Clingfilm, taping the edges of the film to the bottom of the off-cuts with adhesive tape. Place the two core sections into the off-cuts and glue the ends together with epoxy glue. This joint is not very strong but it is only there to hold the two sections together during skinning. What does matter is that the two sections are accurately aligned. This should be guaranteed by using the off-cuts as a base.

The skins are again obechi or balsa; in the case of the latter, 2mm is quite thick enough, because we shall be using glass cloth reinforcing. Naturally, you will be unlikely to find balsa sheets long enough to make the skins in one go, so it is necessary to glue several together. Avoid making the upper and lower skin joints in the same place, for this will cause weak spots. Locate the upper surface joints at the root, for instance, and the lower surface joints at the tip. In addition, alternate the spanwise joints in each skin; the first at the root, the second at the tip, and so on (Fig. 6.11). Make up all four skins - we shall be using a separate LE spar and sand them lightly when the glue has dried.

If epoxy resin is applied directly onto the skins, the balsa will absorb quite a lot of it, which means that you will use more resin than is strictly necessary, and will add excess weight (particularly in the case of high aspect-ratio wings). The balsa will absorb far less resin if you give the inner surface of each skin a coat of dope, or sanding-sealer. This has the additional advantage of preventing the resin from soaking right through the wood and

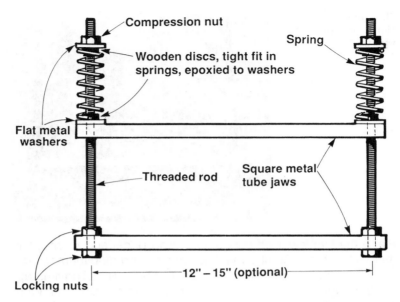

Compression nut

Spring

Wooden discs, tight fit in springs, epoxied to washers

Flat metal washers

Threaded rod

Square metal tube jaws

12" – 15" (optional)

Locking nuts

Fig. 6.13 Spring presses

Calibration of a press, using bathroom scales. Note the pieces of plywood used to protect the scales.

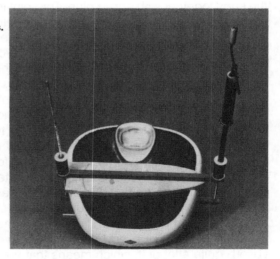

reaching the outer surface, where it would cause hard spots which are difficult to eliminate when sanding the finished wing before covering. Give the doped surfaces a light sanding.

We now have to consider how we are going to hold the skins firmly in contact with the foam core while the resin is setting, a

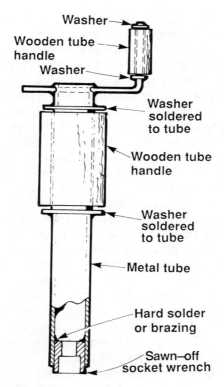

Fig. 6.14 Spring press tightening tool

process which can take anywhere from 5-24 hours, depending on the temperature. There is no instantaneous effect, as with contact glue, and we cannot use a hot iron this time. The answer is to make a sandwich, in the following sequence: lower off-cut, Clingfilm, lower skin, core, upper skin, Clingfilm and upper off-cut (Fig. 6.12). Pressure is then applied to the whole lot while it lies on a perfectly flat surface. There are three ways of doing this, in Chapter 8.

The simplest method is to use spring presses. It is very accurate, since it allows you to vary the pressure according to the width of the wing, thus making possible a very even load. Of course, you will have to make your own presses, but if you are into large-span sailplanes, they are an excellent investment - and not very expensive.

Your local DIY store will provide the necessary square tubing -

3/4in square will do as well as 6 or 7mm threaded rod and appropriate nuts. The best springs are those used as inlet and exhaust valves on car engines, so a visit to the local car breaker is again in order. Pairs of springs should be identical, but they do not all have to be the same. They will have to be calibrated anyway. Figures 6.13 and 6.14 show the construction and the tightening tool, which is necessary if you do not want to skin your knuckles each time you use the presses. If the tube spanner is hardened you will have to grind off the head. When the presses are made - you will need eight, and ten would be even better - you will have to calibrate them. For this, the bathroom scales are ideal. Place two small strips of wood between the metal jaws of the press and the scales, to avoid damaging the latter. Wind the nuts down equally on both sides with the scales trapped between the jaws, until the needle just starts to move. Now wind on an equal number of turns on each side until the scales register a pressure of 10lbs. Stick a strip of paper on one of the jaws and note the number of turns necessary. Now continue for 20lbs, 30lbs, and so on. Depending on the springs used, between 100lbs and 200lbs can be exerted. Make sure that you have identical springs on any one press.

. When you have finished calibrating, the presses are ready for use, but you will first need a couple of flat planks, again to spread the load. It is as well to obtain these planks of the size of the longest wing panels you think you are likely to want to build - this will be 2m, in most cases, allowing the construction of a 4m sailplane. How do we calculate the pressure we need? Let's take as an example a wing panel 55in long, with 9in chord at the root and 5in at the tip. This gives a surface area of 55 x 7 = 385sq. ins. Experience has shown that a good average pressure for skinning white foam is about 2lbs/sq.in. In other words, we need to exert 770lbs of pressure over the whole surface of the panel. We can suppose that we have available 10 presses, each capable of being screwed down to 150lbs. We have, therefore, more than sufficient pressure available. However, if we screw all the presses down to the same amount, we shall be exerting more pressure on the tip than on the root, and there will be a serious danger of squashing the foam so much that it cannot recover its shape, thus losing all the advantages of the carefully-cut aerofoil. A very simple calculation will allow us to spread the load evenly. It goes like this:

Required pressure = $\dfrac{\text{Average pressure (per press)} \times \text{Chord}}{\text{Mean Chord}}$

or, in this specific case:

Root $= \dfrac{77 \times 9}{7} = 99\text{lbs}.$

Tip $= \dfrac{77 \times 5}{7} = 55\text{lbs}.$

All that remains is to work out the pressure to be exerted by each individual press between these two limits. It is done by a simple progression. First take the number of presses to be used, less one, which in our case will be 9. Subtract the lowest pressure previously found from the highest, which gives us 44lbs. Divide this by 9, which comes to 4.88888, let's say 4.9lbs.

The root press is set at 99lbs, the next at 99 - 4.9 = 94.1lbs, the following at 94.1 - 4.9 = 89.2lbs, and so on. In fact, there is no need to be so precise, for there is a lot of leeway, so in practice we can set the presses thus: 99, 94, 89, 84, 79, 74, 69, 64, 59, and 54lbs/sq.in, which will result in the 770lbs being spread quite evenly over the surface. Of course, this supposes a straight taper wing. For a different planform the figures would have to be modified, but this is a simple matter.

The last thing to do before starting work on the skinning is to calculate the amount of resin necessary for one whole wing panel, because you will be skinning both sides at once. A rule of thumb tells us that 1oz of ready-mixed resin will cover 300sq.ins. of sealed balsa - never try to spread the resin on the foam itself, it will flow down into the spaces between the beads, adding useless weight. The figure given is a rough average, but seems to do the trick. If we consider the upper and the lower surfaces, the total area is 770 sq. ins., so we will need 2.3ozs of resin; let's say 2 1/2ozs. Stick very closely to the manufacturer's figures when mixing the two parts, because otherwise there is a risk that the resin will not set. Use a digital kitchen scale, or beg, borrow, or even buy, a letter-scale, which will prove invaluable, not only for mixing resin but for weighing sheets of balsa!

During warm weather the resin should be liquid enough to spread easily, but if you are working in cold conditions it will be

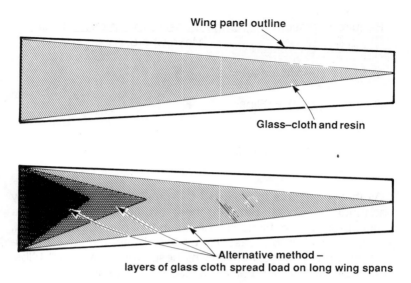

Wing panel outline

Glass–cloth and resin

Alternative method –
layers of glass cloth spread load on long wing spans

Fig. 6.15 Glass-cloth and resin reinforcing

difficult to cover the whole area with the correct amount. In this case, dilute the mixed resin with up to 40% of pure methanol - do not use acetone, which will attack the surface of the foam. If you cannot obtain pure methanol, stand the container of resin in some hot water for approximately five minutes, until it becomes sufficiently liquid for use. 'Hot' means that you can just stand the temperature with your hand. And it you do use methanol, be careful -remember, it's highly flammable.

Using a 1in stiff-bristled brush, spread the resin thinly and evenly all over the sealed side of one of the skins. Next, cut a triangle of 4oz glass cloth, the base of which is equal to the root chord and the height equal to the length of the panel (Fig. 6.15). Lay this on the skin and work resin into it with the brush. You should use just half the amount of resin on this job. Place the lower panel off-cut on one of your two planks, checking that it is completely covered with Clingfilm. Lay the skin, resin side up, on the off-cut, and then place the core on top of the skin.

Prepare the second skin in exactly the same way, but do make sure that you put the resin and glass cloth on the correct side (it is a bit like the two-left-wings syndrome again; think about it before doing it!), and place this on top of the core. Next comes the upper surface off-cut, complete with Clingfilm (don't forget

A wing under pressure. The presses have not yet wound up to the working pressure, bu the sandwich is already held quite firmly.

this film because resin may just creep through the wood in places, and it would otherwise stick the off-cut to the panel!) followed by the other plank.

Finally, slip the presses into place and screw them down to the calculated pressures, and leave the whole thing for at least 24 hours. The panel, planks and presses make up a bulky affair, so the best thing is to put them on a flat floor well out of the way.

It is vital that throughout the process of laying up the different components of the wing, right up to the moment when the presses are screwed down (or the weights put in place) that you check carefully that nothing has moved out of alignment. Check twice - you will find that the resin makes things slide around very easily.

All that is needed to finish the panel is to trim and sand all the edges, and add the LE spar. The result is a strong, light wing panel, which will take a lot of punishment, thanks to the two GRP reinforcing pieces, which spread the load progressively along the wing.

There is an alternative method of calculating the amount of resin needed, and it is one which seems to be a favourite with Continental modellers. It consists of weighing the glass cloth to be used, after it has been cut to size, and then mixing-up the same weight of resin. In practice it works very well, and the method is particularly useful when rounded surfaces, which are difficult to measure, have to be skinned. Once again, be careful to calculate the proportions accurately!

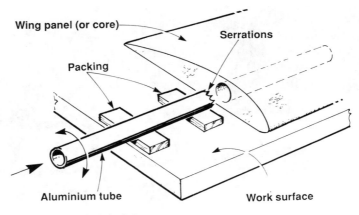

Fig. 6.16 Cutting ballast tube holes in foam cores

Ballast tubes

As we are on the subject of large glider wings, this is the logical place to raise the subject of ballast tubes. Many large gliders, particularly competition models, use ballast to improve penetration in very windy conditions. You can either put it in the fuselage, or in the wings themselves. The former solution imposes a greater than usual strain on the wing-joiners, because they are supporting a greater weight than normal. The more popular choice would seem to be to put the ballast in the wings, which have to carry the extra load in any case, but how can this be done in a wing which has a solid foam core?

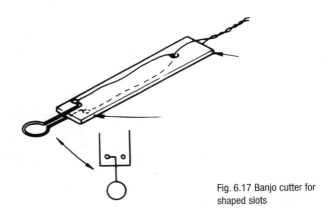

Fig. 6.17 Banjo cutter for shaped slots

Known as a 'Banjo' cutter made from a slightly heavier gauge of ni-chrome wire as a greater degree of rigidity is required, or from stainless wire (often overlooked for hot wire cutters in spite of having a relatively high resistance). It takes the form of a circle with two straight legs, the legs overlapping in the front view (Fig.6.17) the obvious aim being not to short-out the circle. Once having made the cut, the slot formed by the legs can be filled with scrap foam or balsa, however, care must be taken not to distort the section by forcing material into the gap. As the tool can be plunged into the material at any point and run against a non conductive straight edge - short tubes are possible.

7 ALTERNATIVE WING COVERING

Adding lightness

In the previous chapter we examined the three main ways of skinning foam cores, using either obechi or balsa, and contact glue, PVA or epoxy resin. These methods will probably fulfil the needs of most enthusiasts, but we must not neglect other aspects of foam covering, all of which have specific applications.

Very lightweight wings can be made quite simply, not by using a true skin, but by relying on the inherent strength of the structure itself. The most common use for this method is small, electric-powered models, and here blue foam comes into its own. A wing can be cut from blue foam, in the usual way, LE and TE balsa spars added, and covered directly in iron-on film (Fig. 7.1). There will be a great saving in weight, and the panel will be quite strong enough for all normal use, though it will not do to put it in the car with the corner of the tool-box on top of it, for the surface will get dented!

The real limitation with this method is that it is not much use with wings over 40-50in, but it can be used for lightweight slope soarers and small trainers with .09 cu.in. engines. The only tricky bit is getting the iron temperature correct, so you do not melt the foam when applying the film. Your local model shop can advise which film requires the lowest temperature. Even then, it is as well

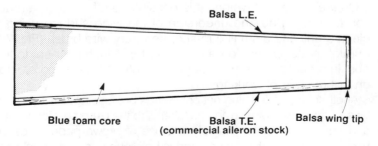

Balsa L.E.

Blue foam core

Balsa T.E.
(commercial aileron stock)

Balsa wing tip

Fig. 7.1 Blue foam core with balsa leading and trailing edges

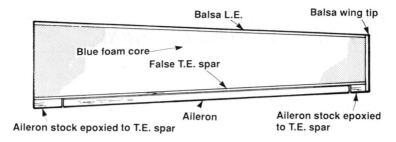

Fig. 7.2 Blue foam core with aileron

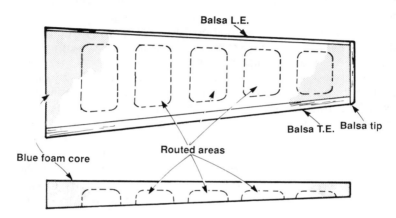

Fig. 7.3 Routing blue foam wing cores

to experiment on scraps of film and foam before covering the model itself. For slightly longer spans, it is as well to go to the trouble of adding a couple of spars, set into the upper and lower surfaces as we have already described. This will give a considerable increase in strength for little added weight (Fig. 7.2).

On the subject of weight, it is possible to effect quite a reduction by routing out the underside of the wing surface using an electric drill and a small cup-shaped rotary wire brush (Fig. 7.3). Enough material should be left every three inches or so, to form ribs, in order to preserve strength. Chapter 11 gives more details on this method of working.

Another way of skinning not only wings but fuselages is that popularised by Chris Golds, who has taken it to the extreme with his huge and complex models - namely, the use of brown paper. It can be used on white and blue foam, and is both cheap and relatively easy to use. In addition, very fine finishes can be obtained by painting.

Cut out the core panels in the usual way, add the LE and TE spars, and any other reinforcements needed. If you are making an aileron-equipped wing, cut out the ailerons and add the appropriate facings now. The wing panel and aileron will be covered separately.

Next you will need some brown wrapping paper, the stuff used for making parcels. If it has been folded, iron the creases smooth. You will see that it has a matt side and a shiny one. Place the paper, shiny side down, on the work surface, put the part to be skinned on top of it, and draw round the outline with a soft pencil. This first skin should be almost exactly the same size as the panel. Turn the panel over, onto its upper surface, repeat the operation, but this time draw the skin about 1in oversize all round. Cut it out.

The glue used for this job is once again white PVA, with colouring added, and diluted with about 30-40% water, to make it easier to spread. It is applied with a 1in wide soft brush. Lay the lower skin, matt side uppermost, on the work surface and cover it with a thin, even coating of the prepared PVA. Do the same for the underside of the foam panel. Now place the skin on the panel, and smooth it into place, using a soft, dry cloth. This is not a difficult process, but try to work quickly, so that the job is finished before the brown paper has time to get soggy. Make sure you get rid of any wrinkles.

When this first skin is in place to your satisfaction, apply glue to the second skin and the upper surface of the panel. Place the skin onto the foam, and smooth down. This time, since you have an oversize skin, you will have an overhang all round. This is

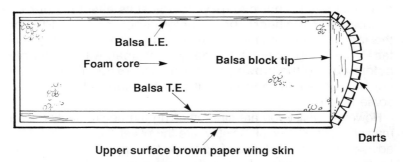

Upper surface brown paper wing skin

Fig. 7.4 Darts in brown paper skins on wing tips

wrapped round the edges of the panel and smoothed onto the lower skin. In order to do this, particularly around curved edges, it will be necessary to cut darts in the paper (Fig. 7.4). This is easy. The edges of the darts will overlap one another. To compensate for the double thickness of these overlaps, go over the area with the brush and a little glue. Check the whole panel to make sure that there are no wrinkles, and then hang the whole thing up to dry. This last part is important. It ensures that both skins dry at the same rate. If they cannot, you will end up with a warped panel.

When the skins are quite dry - give them at least 24 hours in dry weather, more if it is humid - brush over the whole panel with a 50/50 mixture of PVA and water. This layer of glue should be fairly thin so it can penetrate the surface of the paper and dry there, forming a crust, which both strengths the structure and adds to the puncture-resistance of the surface.

For a light-weight panel, you can stop here, give it a coat of paint and one of fuel-proofer, if necessary, and the job is done. If you want a really smooth finish, sand the whole thing down with some 400 grade emery, used dry, and then give it two coats of dope mixed with some talcum powder, sanding between each coat. This will give you a really smooth surface on which to paint. However, remember that this does not add much to the strength of the panel, but there will be an increase in weight.

Join wings of this type in the usual way by first gluing the two panels together, and then wrapping a glass cloth bandage, brushed through with resin, around the joint. Since the foam will be protected by the skins, you can avoid expense by using polyester resin, as sold in car accessory shops. This is quite sufficient, particularly for the smaller wings, but as extra insurance - however psychological its effect might be - you can add a dihedral brace before applying the GRP. For the larger wings, many recommend covering the wing surfaces out to approximately one-quarter span with 1/64in ply before adding the brown paper skin. The extra thickness will not be noticeable, and its limit can be hidden by brushing some glue over it.

However, whilst you are strengthening the centre section, you may also create a weak point where the ply ends, so it would be advisable to use a couple of spars on the upper and lower surfaces in order to spread loads along the wing.

Inset ailerons can be cut out of the finished panel in the usual way, but if you prefer strip ailerons, it will be easier to use trailing edge balsa stock.

Some enthusiasts, having read the foregoing, will probably be tempted to write the method off as 'cheap and nasty'. This would be an error, for it is a very good way of skinning both wings and other parts of a model - Chris Golds' Maxim Gorki, which is 106in span and has eight HGK 20 engines, is totally covered with brown paper!

Instead of brown paper, coloured art card can be wrapped round the core in one piece. This material - which can be obtained at most art supply shops - has a coloured gloss surface on one side, and is matt white on the other. The big advantage is that once the wing has been covered, all that is required is a coat of clear varnish or fuel-proofer. However, the actual skinning operation is slightly delicate. Begin with a foam core to which the balsa LE and TE have been added. On wings up to 50in span, spars are not necessary because the skin is strong.

Lay the card, matt side up, on the work surface, and draw the outline of the skin required with a soft pencil. The skin should be big enough to cover both surfaces in one piece. Lay the core on the card, and mark the point where the balsa TE begins. Roll the core on the card until it is lying on its other surface, and mark the point where the TE finishes. Now draw two parallel lines across the card where the LE will be. The skin will be stuck to the core with epoxy. It is not necessary to use resin. Any slow-curing two-part epoxy will do.

Mix up about 3/4oz of epoxy, and with the aid of a piece of scrap wood or plastic spread it thinly on the matt card, but not at the LE location. Make sure the epoxy is as thin and even as possible. In cold weather, or if the glue is very thick, use a hairdryer to liquefy the epoxy. In between the two lines at the LE position, spread a thin layer of contact glue. Copydex is excellent. Next coat the balsa leading edge of the panel with contact glue. When it is dry, lay the core carefully on the card. Carefully lift the card at the trailing edge, simultaneously pressing the panel down firmly onto the card at the leading edge. Slowly and carefully roll the core, with the card still held against the lower surface, so that the card is brought into contact with the leading edge. Roll it right over until the card is stuck firmly to the balsa LE. Continue until the panel is lying on its upper surface on the epoxied card.

Why must the operation be carried out in this way? If you have spread epoxy over the entire surface of the card, the first thing that will happen is that the core will slide around all over the place. Next, when you start rolling the core on its leading edge, the card will crease in a series of straight lines, instead of mating nicely to the shape of the leading edge. The aerofoil will look awful and performance will be adversely affected. The use of contact glue at the LE avoids these problems. Lastly, lay the skinned panel in its off-cuts, place a large piece of wood on top - ply or chipboard will do - and add weights. Leave the whole thing to dry, on a perfectly flat surface, until the epoxy is thoroughly set. Then take the panel out, and you will have a strong, light wing panel. The explanation is that the epoxy glue will have worked into the matt surface of the card and the foam core, forming a hard crust. This, together with the card and foam, forms a sandwich on both sides of the panel, imparting considerable strength.

Gudy 870

We have considered the traditional glues used in modelling. However, it would not do to ignore the latest developments in hi-tech 'stickology', and the strange name which introduces this section is just that. In the late 1970s a firm in the USA introduced a double-sided tape, called Crazy Tape, which was destined to stick wing skins to cores. Articles were written on the subject, and then it seemed to disappear from the scene - lack of interest?

Recently, I have come across a similar film, developed not for modelling but for industrial photography applications. It is made

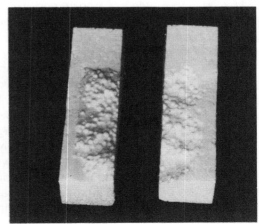

Two Blocks of white foam, stuck together with Gudy 870 and then broken apart almost immediately. The foam, not the joint itself, has failed.

in West Germany by a firm called Hans Neschen GmbH, and it is a quite extraordinary material. First of all, it is very thin, only 40 microns; secondly, the glue is very powerful, and improves with age; thirdly, it comes in a variety of sizes, from narrow tapes right up to a metre in width and in rolls up to 50m. In addition, it is very reasonably priced - at the time of writing around o3.50 per square metre and when you work out how many wings you can cover with this, and the rapidity of use, it is not much more expensive than other glues. However, the most important factor is weight.

One of the elements that adds considerably to the weight of a skinned foam-cored is the glue that is used to fix the skin. In the case of Gudy 870 the weight is negligible, less than 5 gm/sq.m! The glue is an acrylic ester, which is chemically neutral, and which achieves 80% of its tensile strength within 48 hours, but it continues to improve with time.

From this, it can easily be appreciated that for models where weight is an important factor - scale models, electric-powered planes, and so on - this is a real step forward. For instance, one of our Clark Y wing panels, covered with obechi veneer stuck on with Copydex weighs 151gm. The other panel, identical, but using Gudy 870 weighs 137gm. The difference for the whole wing works out at 28gm, or, if you prefer, 1oz. That does not seem an awful lot, perhaps, but when you are trying to cut down on weight, every little helps.

Using Gudy 870 is quite simple, but there are a couple of points to be watched. First, the core must be sanded as smooth as possible, and then either blown across or vacuumed, to remove every possible trace of dust. Place the roll of film on the work surface, with the silicone backing paper underneath, and unroll it. Place the core on the film, and then cut round it with a sharp modelling knife. When you roll up the

It is essential to get rid of any dust before applying Gudy 870.

film, be very careful to brush the backing paper as you do so, because it will pick up dust, which, in turn, will get onto the film.

Place the core, film uppermost, in its off-cut, and rub it all over with the tips of your fingers. Going over it with a hairdryer or heat gun helps greatly to activate the film and make it stick better to the foam. Next, peel off the backing paper. Great care must be taken here, because the film is pure glue, with no support, and it will tend to pull away from the foam in places - remember, it has not polymerised at this stage. If this does happen, push the backing paper back down onto the film and rub it again, very firmly, with your fingertips, then start peeling again. Incidentally, I have found that the best results are obtained when the backing paper is pulled off at an angle of 45 deg to the line of the panel, and when the angle where it comes away from the film is kept as sharp as possible.

Once the backing has been removed, take the sanded and dusted skin and lay it carefully in place on the core, in the same way as if you were using contact cement. When it is in position, rub it firmly all over, to ensure maximum contact, and the job is done. The resulting panel is every bit as strong as one made with contact cement, but a lot lighter.

Naturally skinning wings is not the only use that can be found for Gudy 870 in building. Perhaps one of its most useful properties is that it can be cut very easily with the HWC when it is freshly applied. For instance, the forward hollowed-out turtle-deck of the fuselage made from blue foam in Chapter 11 uses this technique. Not having a piece of foam wide enough to cover the fuselage

A large cowl made from blue foam blocks stuck together with Gudy 870. The glue joints are perfectly flush after sanding.

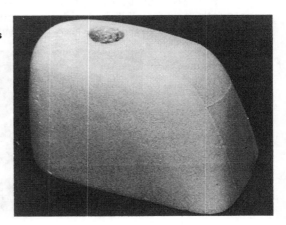

width in one go, I simply stuck two pieces together with Gudy 870 put the templates in place, and then cut the deck with the HWC.

Since I had not taken any precautions over the glue line, the HWC had to cut through the adhesive film. Neither my 'No.2' nor I felt the slightest resistance to the movement of the wire as it sliced through the glued area.

Be careful! Once freshly-applied film has completely poly-merised, there will be some resistance to the cutter. The second point is that there will still be a change of texture at the glue line when it comes to sanding, so only use this technique where the finished HWC cut is the surface, and there is no need of sanding. Thirdly, don't throw away small blocks of blue foam. Keep them in a scrap-box; you can stick them together to make larger pieces, using Gudy 870 thus effecting a saving in costs.

I have used Gudy 870 to stick thin ply doublers to the main fuselage sides, at nose and wing seat positions, with no signs of weakness. There is no doubt in my mind that the whole fuselage could be skinned in this way, as could floats. In fact, there seems to be little limit to the applications possible - how long will it be before someone builds a whole plane in this way? All joking apart, this adhesive film is a boon to modellers building electric-powered planes, where weight is at a premium, as well as to scale buffs, who could use it for adding lightness. All in all, a very satisfactory material, of which we should hear more in the future.

Note: In the UK Gudy 870 can only be obtained from the follow-ing address:

Hans Neschen Ltd.,
8, Titan Way,
Lichfield,
Staffs.
WS14 9TT

Telephone 01543 255411

8 GRP SKINS

Application

It cannot be denied that the so-called GRP wing offers by far the finest finish available to us, and it is also the one which reproduces the most accurately that of full-size sailplanes. Continental modellers are very keen on this type of construction, and German manufacturers excel at it - but take a look at the prices for this kind of model, and you may have a shock! They are very, very expensive. Quite a few modellers, on the other hand, would like to own a model with wings like these. Well, by using foam cores, it is quite possible to make them yourself.

In point of fact, there are two methods available to us, one of which is what might be called a bit of a cheat. Instead of making the wing with a true GRP skin, you construct it as previously described with obechi, and a GRP reinforcement. Sand everything down until you have got the best possible finish on the surface. When this is done, take some lightweight glass cloth - most model shops sell it, and it is available in grades from 1/2 to 1 oz./sq. yd. Cut a piece corresponding to the size of the panel surface, lay it in place, and then go over the whole thing with your stiff-bristled brush and some very liquid resin. Make sure that the whole surface is thoroughly wetted - when glass cloth is correctly wetted, it assumes a faintly translucent appearance. Check that there are no air bubbles anywhere. These show up as somewhat opaque areas. Chase them out towards the edges of the panel, where they will escape. Be scrupulous about this, because you are going to rub the surface down afterwards, and if you leave bubbles, you will quickly rub through the GRP where they occur, creating little holes which will have to be repaired.

When the resin has set, but whilst it is still 'green' (that is to say, it has solidified, but is still slightly flexible), run a sharp-edged cutter blade right round the panel, taking off the excess, but being careful not to cut the panel itself. Turn it over, and do the same thing on the other side. It is a good idea to wrap this second layer round the LE. The overlapping joint can be feathered out when rubbing down.

When the resin has completely polymerised, after a minimum of 24 hours, out with the emery paper and start rubbing down. Use 400 grade paper wet, with a few drops of washing-up liquid in the water to provide lubrication. Don't apply too much pressure. Once the surface is free from any nasties, change to 600 grade emery, used in the same way. You will get a reasonable surface in this way, but it will probably have quite a few imperfections. These can be dealt with by mixing some micro-balloons in a little resin to form a paste, and then smearing the latter onto the surface. Rub down again. You should now have a good surface, but it may have a lot of pin-holes in it. Give the whole panel a good coat of white emulsion paint, and then rub nearly all of it off. Do this again, if necessary, and your wing should be ready for painting. Do check for compatibility of the paints first!

Vacuum bag

This method gives good results, and indeed is popular with British modellers, but it has to be said that it is not a true GRP wing, being rather a mixture of two things. Some modellers will want to make the real McCoy, so we will take a look at the method. It is based on moulding in a vacuum bag, so the first thing you will have to do is to find yourself a vacuum pump. This is not expensive, as we have hinted at already, because literally thousands of perfectly good, working pumps are thrown away every month all over the country. These are the pumps used in household refrigerators and freezer units. Get hold of a fairly big one, which will stand up to continuous use better than a small one.

Most pumps look like oversized iron eggs, with several tubes sticking out of them. It is an easy matter to find out which tube you want. Just stick your finger over the end of each, while the pump is running, and when your finger sticks to one of them, that's the one you want!

The motor works in an oil bath, but even then, if it is allowed to run for any length of time, it will get pretty hot; and some will even give up the ghost altogether if run without stopping. It is therefore necessary to find a way of switching the pump off from time to time. Once more, no hi-tech stuff; the accessory just could not be more simple. It consists of the pressure capsule attached to the distributor of most cars in order to provide an automatic advance

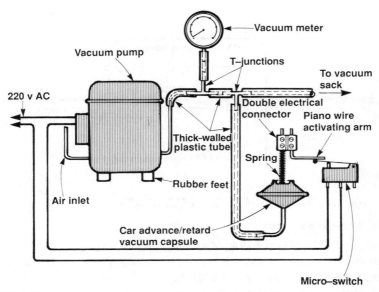

Fig. 8.1 Vacuum pump

and retard, plus a 240 volt micro switch. The first can be found extremely cheaply at the car breaker's, the second from most Tandy shops (Fig. 8.1). The method is simplicity itself. As the pump creates a higher and higher vacuum, the diaphragm in the capsule draws the arm down further and further, until it activates the micro-switch, thus switching off the pump. As soon as the inevitable air leaks in the system allow the arm to creep back up a little, pushed by the spring, the micro-switch will bring the pump back into action, and so the cycle goes on. Of course, the fewer leaks there are, the less work the pump will have to do.

The wiring might prove slightly tricky for some people. Essentially, you will find that the incoming mains leads has three wires, blue, brown and yellow/green. The latter goes to a tag on the metal container, and should not be touched. The blue and brown wires will go to a tag strip, on which there is a series of other, variously-coloured wires. The blue from the mains goes straight across the tag board, through a small black box and on into a terminal in a plug on the compressor housing - do not touch this wire at any point. The brown wire goes to one terminal on the board, and apparently leaves it on another, with no connection between the two. In the refrigerator installation a thermo-

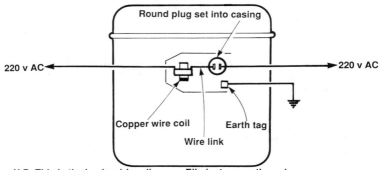

Fig. 8.3 Vacuum pump wing

stat switch made the link. You must take a wire from the brown mains lead to one side of your micro-switch, and then another from the other side of the switch back to the other brown wire on the tag board, which eventually ends up, like the blue, on a terminal in the plug in the compressor casing. Lastly, get rid of all the wires that are doing nothing (Fig. 8.2). Warning: 240 volts mains electricity is not a thing to be treated lightly. The operation described is quite simple, especially if you check what you are doing with a voltmeter. However, if you have any doubts about your ability to carry out the modification, don't do it! In the first place, you may ruin the compressor; and second, you can give yourself a nasty shock, or worse! Find a competent friend (really competent, not an armchair pilot) or, failing that, go to your local electricity repair man. It will take him five minutes, and thus won't cost much. It's much better to pay a couple of pounds and be sure, than to find out the nasty way that you are no electrician.

You now have a basic working vacuum pump, but it is a good idea to add that most useful accessory, a vacuum meter, which measures in millimetres of mercury. No hi-tech device, and to be found in any car accessory shop, it is used for measuring the depression in the inlet manifold of car engines. The reason for fitting it is not swank, but because it is really useful. Until you have played around with this method, you will not realise just how much pressure can be exerted by a vacuum bag. It is quite astonishing. Tests have shown that at over 400mm/Hg, white foam will be compressed to the point of irreparable crunching.

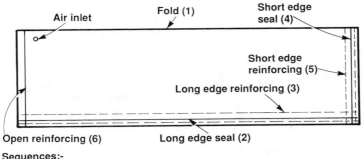

Sequences:-
1. Fold plastic sheet in half lengthwise
2. Tape long edge
3. Reinforce long edge tape
4. Tape one short edge
5. Reinforce short edge tape
6. Reinforce second short edge
   – do not seal opening
7. Fit air outlet

Length: half–span + 6" – 8"
Width: chord + 3" – 4"

Fig. 8.3 Vacuum sack

The pump you have made will go up above 650-700mm/Hg! You therefore need a way of checking the level of vacuum you are using.

To connect it all up, buy some plastic tubing with fairly thick walls - the sort used for aquariums is ideal - and a couple of T-connectors from the same source, and hook it all up as shown.

You are now almost in business, but not quite. You still need the plastic bag into which everything is put. It is unlikely that you will be able to find a ready-made one of the dimensions you require, so you will have to make it yourself. Buy some fairly thick plastic sheeting - the garden centre is your best source - and a big roll of 3in, or wider, sticky tape.

Let us suppose that you want to make a wing panel 60 x 9in. For this, your bag should measure at least 70 x 15in. Cut a piece of plastic 70 x 30in, fold it along its length, and join the two long edges with the tape (Fig. 8.3). You will find this operation quite tricky, and a second pair of hands will be helpful - preferably someone with dressmaking experience, but not absolutely necessary. Work on a large surface, it is easier. Pull oft sufficient tape to do the whole joint and lay it sticky side up on the work-surface, taking care to weight the ends, or it will immediately coil up on itself! Lay the edge of the plastic sheet on half the width of the tape, ensuring that the plastic is pulled tight at both ends, or you will get wrinkles, which are potential sources of leaks. Lay the other edge of the plastic on the first one, pull tight, and fold the tape over and stick

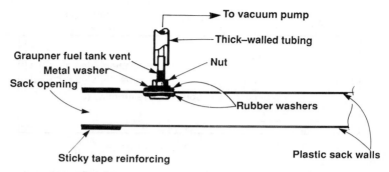

Fig. 8.4 Vacuum sackair outlet

down. It is an excellent idea to use a second length of tape on each side, overlapping, to increase the surface of the joint.

Do exactly the same thing at one end of the bag; this end remains permanently sealed, as does the long edge. You now have a bag with one open end, into which you will eventually insert the core to be skinned.

Now you need a way of connecting the tubing from the compressor to the bag. This is always a weak point in the system. There is, however, a relatively simple solution; you will need one of the metal inlet tubes used on Graupner fuel tanks - it has a shoulder at one end, a threaded portion and a nut. Figure 8.4 explains all, but do not be tempted to over tighten the nut, for it will crush the rubber washers and spoil the seal.

Since you will wish to use the bag over and over again, it is advisable to reinforce the edges of the opening with strips of tape. Then, when you peel off the strip used for actually sealing the bag, it will not deform the plastic sheeting.

Vacuum system tests

Since everything is now ready for use, a trial run is in order. It is better to discover the faults, if any, now, rather than spoil a wing and a lot of resin and glass cloth! You will need a sheet of 5mm. plywood, and it is a good idea to round off all the edges, and to put a radius on the corners, in order to avoid making punctures in the vacuum bag. In addition, since there is a possibility of resin dropping on the wood, it is also useful to cover the whole thing with a sheet of the same plastic you used for making the bag - fix it underneath with sticky tape, so that it is tight, and cannot move. (Because I build sailplane wings of up to 5 metre span, I use a

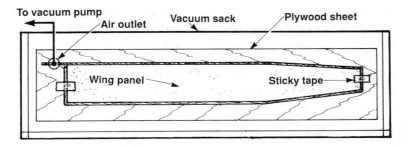

Fig. 8.5 Layout of components in sack

2.5m bag, and a sheet of ply 2.4m x 34cm, the same outfit being used for all sizes of wings.) When your bag and ply sheet are ready, attach the trial block of foam to the ply with two pieces of double-sided tape - not thick, Vibration-absorbing servo tape, but the very fine type meant for sticking down fitted carpets. Now place a thick piece of nylon cord, about 6mm diameter, all round the block, as close to the base as possible. This will provide a passage from the extremities of the bag to the air outlet. If you do not fit this, then air will be trapped in parts of the bag with no way of getting out, and the vacuum will be only partial. This will result in uneven pressure on the foam, and the system will not work properly.

Slide the ply sheet into the bag, and arrange it so that the air outlet tube is resting on the end of the nylon cord. Now seal the end of the bag, using sticky tape as before, making sure that the seal is hermetic (Fig. 8.5). Connect up the pump, and switch on. The pump will run for two or three minutes, depending on the amount of air in the bag, and then will stop. Check the pressure, and set the micro-switch activating arm so that the pump will give a vacuum of about 250mm/Hg, which is quite sufficient for white foam.

The pump will work for a few seconds, and then stop. The needle on the gauge will drop slowly, and when it has gone down about 100mm/Hg, will cut in again. This range is quite normal, and is caused by the micro-switch spring operation. The time interval between the pump shutting down and then switching on can vary according to your system. I had one bag which would last three minutes, but the current one will only last 45 seconds. It all depends on how well it is made. Do not worry about it. Provided your pump is off for at least 25-30 seconds, everything is OK, because it will be running at a ratio of 10:1, and even after 12-14 hours it will hardly be warm to the touch. Naturally, if it will not switch off for more than a few seconds, you obviously have a leak somewhere, so start listening hard, and when you locate it, out with the sticky tape and patch it up.

If you cannot obtain a vacuum meter - most unlikely - then you will have to experiment until you find the right pressure. There is very little help to be offered here. Go to a point where the foam is permanently distorted, and work back from there.

The Skinning Process

We can assume that you have cut the foam cores - and joined the core and off-cut panels, in the case of a two-section panel. Sand down to a very smooth surface, add the joiner tube or strip - see Chapter 10 - plus the root rib, made of 2-3mm plywood. Sand this down again.

The method involves skinning the upper surface of the panel in one operation, and then starting again and skinning the other. Cover the lower surface off-cut with Clingfilm, which is taped in place. Fix the core to it with three pieces of double-sided tape, and then use the same tape to fix the whole thing to the ply sheet; then put it all to one side.

The next bit is very important. In order to make the wing, you will use the vacuum bag to press down on the laminated surface, holding it flat while the resin is curing. The finished surface of the wing, therefore, depends entirely on the material that is used directly on top of the resin and cloth lay-up, and the wall of the sack will not do! It is very thin and supple, and will conform to every single imperfection present on the wing surface. The result would be a skin full of humps and hollows and wrinkles. What is needed is a special sheet of thick plastic which has a certain rigidity, sufficient not to follow all these little imperfections, but rather to even them out. At the same time, it must be flexible enough to follow the form of the aerofoil. Finally, it must be made of a plastic which will not stick to the finished surface! A tall order, and the only material that I know of which fulfils all three criteria is polyethylene sheeting, about 0.6mm thick. This is ideal, and needs no waxing before use. Try the garden centre and builders' suppliers. The thickness can vary, but it should not be less than 0.5mm and not more than 1 mm, for obvious reasons. If you cannot obtain polyethylene, try nylon or PVC, but here it will be necessary to give the sheeting a good waxing to ensure that it does not stick to the polymerised wing surface. Do not use a silicone wax!

The plastic sheet should now be cut to the exact planform of the wing, plus 3mm at the leading and trailing edges, having made due allowance for the curvature of the surface. The length should be exactly that of the core.

Since you are going to cover the upper surface first, decide which side of the sheet is which, and lay it face up on the work surface. Now, with a roller, give it a coating of vinyl (water-based) white emulsion, the sort used generally for painting ceilings. This first coat will be full of holes, since the paint has a job maintaining film coherence on such a slippery surface, and will break up. When it is quite dry, give it a second coat; this time the whole surface will be covered. Leave to dry.

The paint is there to avoid the formation of the tiny holes seen so often on epoxy mouldings, even when a gel-coat is used. The resin penetrates the paint completely, giving a brilliant white finish with absolutely no holes at all. Why this should be is beyond me; sufficient to say, the method works.

The next job is to mix up your resin and spread it on the sheet. To calculate the amount of resin necessary, the generally accepted method is to cut up the glass cloth to size, weigh it, and then mix up exactly the same weight of resin. This works very well. Measure the resin and hardener as accurately as possible, and there will be no problem with correct polymerisation. (One big advantage of epoxy over polyester, apart from the higher cost, is that it does not smell, which can be very useful when you have to work in the house!) Spread the mixed resin evenly over the painted plastic, being careful not to lift the paint. You should aim at spreading three-quarters of the resin on the sheet, and this is quite easy, with a bit of practice. Use a medium 2in. brush for the spreading.

You now need to know what glass cloth to use, and this is another of those subjects that give rise to a lot of debate. First of all, there are three types of cloth, ordinary woven, bi-directional and uni-directional. There are minor variations on these themes, but we can ignore them. The ordinary cloth is suitable for non-stressed finishing - such as the previously described covering on balsa or obechi. Bi-directional, distinguished by a square weave, as opposed to diagonal in the case of the ordinary cloth, is suitable for most purposes. Uni-directional has most of the fibres running in one direction, and some experts swear by it for wings. It is sometimes difficult to find, and more expensive. I use bi-directional most of the time, and ordinary cloth when I cannot obtain it; and I have yet to experience a structural failure which could be blamed on the type of cloth.

The second point is the thickness, or rather weight, of cloth to be used. This, again, is a tendentious subject, there being as many opinions as builders. I can only offer the specifications that have worked for me, which are:

1. Up to 2.50m (100in.) span, thermal soarers: one layer of 4oz and one of 1 oz cloth.
2. Up to 2.50m (100in.) span, aerobatic: one layer of 4oz and one of 3oz.
3. 3m (120in.) span, thermal soarers: one layer of 4oz and one of 2oz.
4. 4m (150in.) span, thermal soarers: two layers of 4oz.
5. x5m (200in.) span, thermal soarers: one layer of 5oz and one of 4oz, plus reinforcement.

Having said that, a bit of common sense is necessary. If you want to fly around sedately, with no violent manoeuvres, then the weights shown are adequate. If, on the other hand, you are given to moments of exuberance and throw the model around a bit (like me!), then some reinforcing is necessary. We will come to that in a moment.

Using the polyethylene sheet as a pattern, cut out the glass cloth, to the exact size of the sheet. Lay the thinner cloth onto the resined plastic, and, either with the flat of the hand or a brush, work it out so that it lies evenly on the sheet. Take your time; there is no hurry. Get it right - completely flat. You will see it beginning to change colour slightly as the resin starts to wet it. Go over the whole surface with a stiff brush, jabbing down vertically - but gently - until all is wet. Then lay on the thicker cloth, and repeat the process. You may have to use a tiny bit of the remaining resin to wet the cloth all over, but if you do, use as little as possible. The more resin you use, the heavier your wing will be, and it will not be any stronger! You may think that there is not enough resin; but there is. The pressure in the vacuum bag will finish the wetting process, and squeeze the resin out of the cloth and into contact with the foam.

If you think that you do need some reinforcement, now is the moment to do something about it. The easiest solution is to use some carbon tape, 1 in. wide for medium-span wings, and 2in. for larger ones. It should be laid on the glass cloth at a point corresponding to the maximum thickness of the aerofoil section. This is sufficient for most purposes. We will see what can be done for the really high-performance models a little later on.

The lay-up in place in the sack, ready to be sealed. Note the nylon cord, which runs all round the block, and which will go under the air outlet.

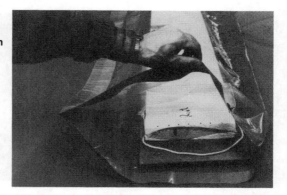

Sealing the sack with three-inch sticky tape. The cord is located exactly under the air outlet - if it isn't, you will have problems pumping all the air out.

You still have a little resin left in your pot, and now is the time to use it. Spread it evenly, with the brush, along the leading and trailing edges of the foam core, in a band about ¢in. wide. This is to make doubly sure that these edges are securely stuck down to the foam.

The next job is slightly tricky if you are on your own, so it might be as well to recruit an extra pair of hands. (Don't worry if you can't, it is possible to manage single-handed, but it's just a little more difficult.) Pick up the polyethylene sheet and turn it over onto the foam core, so that the laid-up glass cloth is between the sheet and the foam. Then move the whole thing around - very gently -until the edge of the sheet overhangs the LE of the core by 2-3mm. This is most important. If you get the LE wrong, the wing will be ruined, so take your time and get it exactly right. When you are satisfied, use two small pieces of sticky tape to fix the sheet in place at the root and the tip. They should run span-wise from the sheet down onto the ply. Check everything again. Now spread a sheet of Clingfilm over the whole lot, to avoid any

This shot shows the lay-up which will go into the sack - core, polyethylene sheet, off-cuts and plastic-covered ply base.

resin that may get squeezed out from coming into contact with the vacuum bag (there shouldn't be any, if you have used the correct amount of resin).

Place the nylon cord around the base of the block, slide the whole thing into the vacuum bag, seal the end, hook up the pump, and start it (Fig. 8.6). As the vacuum pressure builds up, check constantly that as the walls of the sack press down on the polyethylene sheet, they do not move it. If this does happen - and it may - there must be no hesitation. Stop the pump, open the bag and re-align. This is a bit of a bind, but much better than having a ruined wing! At last, everything is in place, the pump is working correctly, and all that remains is to wait. How long? That will depend on the type and make of resin, and the temperature in the room where the wing is drying. It can vary between nine and twenty-four hours. As a control, use a tiny bit of the resin mix on scraps of glass cloth - the same as that used to lay-up the wing - placed on a piece of balsa beside the vacuum bag. When the sample is polymerised, you will know that the GRP on the wing is well set and can be taken out. When you inspect the surface that

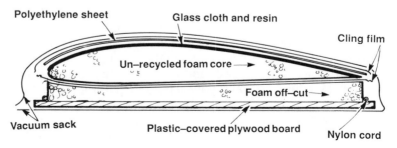

Fig. 8.6 Lay-up of upper surface of GRP wing

The skinning process under way - the sack has pressed down on the lay-up, and crinkled around the edges. The meter is showing 180 mm/mg. and dropping. The switch will cut in again at about 140mm.

you have created, you will see, first of all, that you have a shiny, white surface with no pin-holes in it. The LE and TE will have some 'flash' which can be removed with a cutter blade and sanding. You may find that there is some wing-tip deformation if the polyethylene sheet has crushed down the unsupported foam at the extremity of the panel. The answer to this is to cut panels at least 1 in. longer than actually required, and then reduce them after the laying-up process. At the root there should be no crushing, since the ply rib will have taken all the pressure.

Lay-up the upper surface of the second panel, and go through the whole thing again. You then have to prepare the lower surface. Now is the time to install the control runs, whether they be cable or pushrod. Put one panel in its upper off-cut - upside-down -and cut out the control-run, as described in Chapter 5. Then plug the channel with scraps of foam, and sand it down to the original surface. If you do not do this, you will end up with a shallow depression of the shape of this run, after the glassing process.

The LE needs some special treatment in order to consolidate it. When the upper surface skin has been sanded to conform to the foam core, take a broken piece of hacksaw-blade and run it down the core, immediately behind the LE, to create a shallow channel between the GRP skin and the foam. The last bit of preparation is to run a length of adhesive tape along the upper surface of the panel, immediately behind the LE. This is intended to protect the surface from any resin which may run out of the lay-up and onto this finished surface (Fig. 8.7).

With the off-cut stuck on the ply sheet, the panel in the off-cut, the glass cloth cut and the resin mixed, you are ready to lay-up

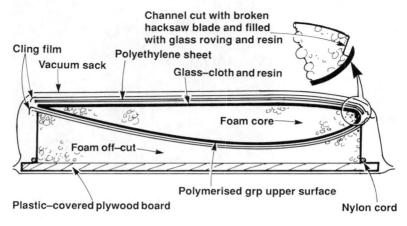

Fig. 8.7 Lay-up of lower surface of GRP wing

the under surface. The first thing is to run a little resin into the channel you have cut at the leading edge. Pull out three or four strands of glass from your main sheet of cloth - the one from which you cut the skins - and lay them in the channel, making sure they are tapped down well. If you need a lot of strength here, you can use carbon tows, or even kevlar. A cheap source of kevlar tows is a ship's chandler, where you can buy a couple of metres of Kevlar cord, which can then be unravelled to provide tows.

You can now lay-up the rest of the panel just like the upper side. Cover it with the polyethylene, Clingfilm, check the LE and nylon cord; and into the bag. A few hours later, all being well, out comes the wing, complete except for the tip. A short length of the deformed section is sawn off, a balsa block glued on and shaped, covered in GRP and sanded to blend in to the rest of the panel. The panel is now ready to have the aileron - if any - installed in the usual way, after which it can be sanded down and painted; and it is ready for use.

Foam choice

It is most annoying to find a wing which, when taken out of the vacuum bag, has an apparently lovely surface, but when examined closely from certain angles is found to have a series of almost imperceptible humps and hollows all along its length. It took a while to find out why, but it all comes down to the foam itself. For this particular type of construction, you must avoid recycled foam! The hard spots in it stand up better to the pressure of the polyethylene sheet than the others, and it is this which gives rise to the tiny deformations. I have already said that it is extremely difficult to know if a sheet of foam is recycled or not. There is, however, one test that helps a lot. When you buy the foam, feel the surface of the sheet. If it has a granular feel - similar to that of a panel which has been cut with the HWC too hot - then there is a pretty fair chance that this is recycled. In any case, avoid it for GRP wing panels. If, on the other hand, the surface is very smooth and soft, rather like the surface of a correctly-cut panel, then the foam should be fine. Of course, if you use blue foam, you will not have this problem, but you will be adding extra weight.

It may necessary, on the bigger models, or those used for competition work, to add some reinforcement besides the carbon tape. This is more likely on white foam, which has less compression resistance than blue. It is compression forces that may cause the damage. The accepted system is to add a full-depth spar at the point of maximum thickness. This can be done by cutting the core sections lengthwise, as already described. There is an even better way. Lay-up and leave the upper surface to cure. Turn it over and put the panel in the off-cut. Now, using double-sided tape, stick a long metal straight-edge on the core, at the point where the spar is required. With the hacksaw blade, cut a slot for the spar, going right down to the inside to the upper surface GRP. The spar itself can be thin plywood (2mm), or a built-up spar of balsa, with the grain of the wood running vertically (don't forget we are reinforcing against vertical compression forces). This last method will allow you to build up a spar which progressively reduces in thickness, thus affording a degree of load spreading. When laying up the lower surface, drop some resin into the slot, push the spar into place, and then lay-up in the usual way.

Upmarket wings
Many people raise arguments against this kind of wing, although I rather suspect that the arguments are sometimes to hide a case of sour grapes. Full-size gliders use this kind of structure almost exclusively now, and their performances speak for themselves, as do those of the high-performance West German models. I have costed the GRP wings for a 3m glider. Taking into consideration all the materials, including vacuum bag, sticky tape et al,

the air of panels, ready to use, came to just under £30 at the time of writing. Compare that with commercial prices! Another argument is that they take a long time to make. With forward planning and a bit of common sense, the same two panels were cut, laid-up and installed in a week of evenings! The result: gleaming, up-market glass wings, which have an excellent performance - try them!

9 THE LASER METHOD

Ribs from foam

It must not be thought that the only way foam can be used for wings is as a solid core. Not so. Blue foam can be used to make a wing which resembles a traditional one, built up from balsa ribs and spars, but instead of using expensive balsa wood, we can cut the ribs from a block of foam.

There are three ways of doing this. The first is to use the HWC to slice up sheets of blue foam of the required thickness, and then cut out the ribs in the usual way, using a modelling knife and a template. The second is to count the number of ribs you need, add 1mm per rib to allow for the loss of foam from melting as the HWC goes through, cut a block and turn it into the shape of the ribs using templates and the HWC. All that then remains to do is to slice off the individual ribs from the block (Fig. 9.1).

What is the Laser method?

Both methods are perfectly feasible and adequate, and, in the case of a fairly large wing, do represent a substantial saving in money. However, there are no other advantages. The Laser method, on the other hand, has one very big plus factor, in that it is impossible, if carried out correctly, to build a warped wing panel. The method was invented, or developed, in the USA specifically in order to make wings for aerobatic models for the new, Aresti-style manoeuvres, where light weight is very important, not to mention accurate panels.

Blue foam is used for the construction, because it is denser, and thus stronger, than the white variety. The method at first seems long and complicated, but this is not so, providing you progress in a logical and orderly manner. With a bit of pre-planning, a pair of wing panels can be built as rapidly, as light and more cheaply than a similar pair using balsa.

The basis of the method is that the panels are built from foam rib blanks which are stuck vertically on a flat building board, and then cut out in situ with the use of templates and the HWC. The method can be adapted to build wings from existing plans, to suit your own designs or to replace existing wings. It is most useful for

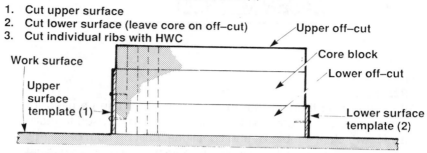

Fig. 9.1 Cutting blue foam ribs with the HWC

power models of over 60in. span, because it is at these sizes that we start to see appreciable cost savings over the use of balsa for the ribs. The finished structure is as strong as, if not stronger than, a balsa wing. I have personally – and involuntarily – put this to the test with my Bigfoot, an 80in. glider tug, when the fuselage was damaged beyond repair thanks to a flat receiver battery; the wing suffered really minor damage, which was quite repairable.

Technique

You will need two building boards, slightly larger than the wing panels you wish to make. If chosen well oversize, these boards will do for any future wings of this type that you may wish to construct. They can be of practically any material, but must be perfectly flat, because upon this depends the accuracy of the finished wing. I use chipboard, which is quite adequate, but the ideal is to use an old, white formica shelf, cut in two. Because it is laminated it will be more likely to remain flat, and marking-out is very easy on this surface.

No plan is used. Instead, the rib positions are marked on the building board with a felt pen. Start with a central reference line, running spanwise through the centre of the root and tip chords. From this, draw in the LE and TE lines (in the case of the former, do not forget to compensate for the thickness of the LE spar, which, typically, will be of ⅜in. hard balsa). Now draw in the rib stations (Fig. 9.2). As a rule of thumb, on an 80in. wing I position ribs every 3in, which has proved quite sufficient. Once again, beware of the 'two-left-wings' syndrome; mark the LE and the wing root clearly on your board!

Cut to size a blue foam block of the required thickness (this will depend on the thickness of the chosen aerofoil, but you should

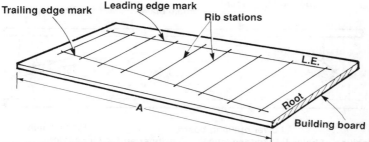

Trailing edge mark   Leading edge mark

Rib stations

L.E.

A

Root

Building board

N.B. Distance 'A' must be at least 1" less than the length of the HWC

Fig. 9.2 Marking out building board

allow at least ½in. extra above and below the ribs) and long enough to cut out the required number of rib blanks. It is always a good idea to reduce wingtip inertia as far as possible; and as the stress on any given wing decreases towards the tip, these factors should be taken into consideration when deciding on the thickness of the ribs. Every little helps. I use three root ribs ⁹⁄₁₆in. thick, four of ⁵⁄₁₆in. and four tip ribs of ³⁄₁₆in. Use these figures as guidelines. Ribs a little thicker will not add much weight, but I would not advise going any thinner.

The rib blanks, once cut, must be spot-glued to the building board on their stations and with the ends accurately aligned at the LE (Fig. 9.3). The easiest way to do this is to fix a metal straight edge along the LE line, and then butt the ends of the blanks up against it. Any rapid-setting glue can be used for fixing the blanks. I use fast PVA. One very important (and timesaving) point is to get the blanks standing absolutely vertical on the board. This will mean that when you come to fit the spar-webbing, all you have to do is chop up pieces of foam with square ends. If the blanks are not vertical, you will need to cut each piece of webbing individually

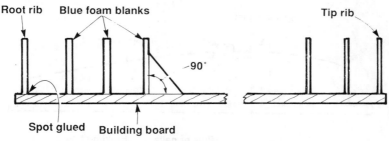

Root rib   Blue foam blanks   Tip rib

90°

Spot glued   Building board

N.B. Note decreasing thickness of rib blanks from root to tip

Fig. 9.3 Setting up foam blanks

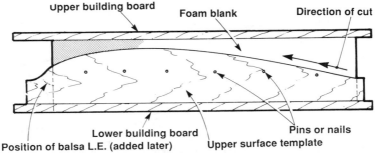

Upper building board   Foam blank   Direction of cut

Lower building board   Pins or nails

Position of balsa L.E. (added later)   Upper surface template

Fig. 9.4 End view of building board and foam blanks, ready to cup upper surface

A selection of templates. From the top, spars; dihedral brace and undercarriage template.

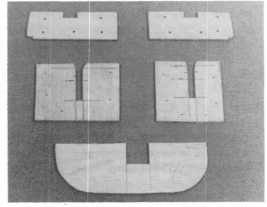

to the required angle. A small set-square can be made from a piece of scrap wood.

When the glue is dry, pin the *upper* surface templates to the end ribs, in the usual way (double templates are almost imperative for this method), put spots of glue on the top edge of the blanks, and place the second building board on top, being careful to align it

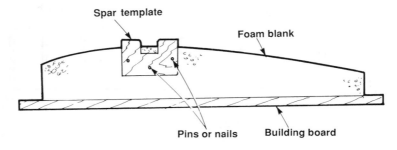

Spar template   Foam blank

Pins or nails   Building board

Fig. 9.5 Cutting spar slots

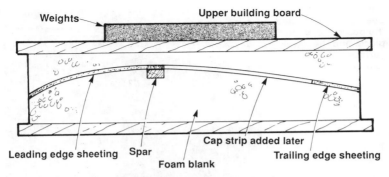

Weights — Upper building board

Leading edge sheeting — Spar — Foam blank — Cap strip added later — Trailing edge sheeting

Fig. 9.6 Gluing spar and leading and trailing edge sheeting

vertically with the bottom one (Fig. 9.4). When the glue is dry, make the upper surface cut with the HWC.

Lift off the top board – which will soon become the cradle for the wing when you come to work on the underside – and put it somewhere safe! Using small templates fixed securely to the end ribs, cut out the upper surface spar slots (Fig. 9.5). On a wing of this size I use $\frac{3}{8} \times \frac{1}{8}$in. spruce. Using the spar as a guide, adjust the slots with a knife, if necessary, so that the spar sits flush with the surface of the ribs. Glue it in place – and if you intend to use the model on water, be careful to choose waterproof glue. I speak from sad experience! Next, glue on the LE sheeting and the split TE using the other board, loaded with weights, to hold the sheeting in place while the glue dries. Follow these with the rib cap strips, which are 1in. wide. All the sheeting on an 80in. wing can be from $\frac{1}{16}$in. (2mm) balsa (Fig. 9.6). Give the whole thing a brisk sanding, and then, using only two glue spots on each rib position, place the second building board back in place. While the glue is drying, fit the *lower* surface templates, and then make the second cut. Lift

Using the templates and the HWC to cut the channels for the wing spar.

The top surface has been cut and sheeted, the board tacked in place, and the lower surface cut is about to begin.

off the top building board, turn it over, and you will see that the wing, upside down, is now safely held flat for work on the second side. This, of course, is the whole idea of the exercise – it avoids warps.

Cut the spar slots, trial fit – without glue – and then cut out and adjust the spar webbing from blue foam, and sand each piece accordingly. Glue the whole lot in place, followed by the spar, and place some weights along its length. Then cut the dihedral brace slot as required, but do not glue the brace in place yet!

Now stop, and think! If you are going to use outboard ailerons, now is the time to fit the snake or pushrod runs, just forward of the spar – a job that cannot be done once the undersurface LE sheeting is in place. If, like me, you use 2mm piano wire in Kavan golden outers actuating 90-degree bellcranks, the job is most easily done by drawing a series of marks in a straight line on the edges of the ribs where the outer is to go, and the boring the holes, starting from the root, with a length of 3mm outside diameter brass

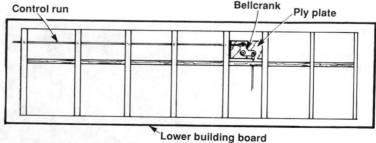

N.B. Wing panel in this figure is upside down on lower building board

Fig. 9.7 Aileron control installation

This shot shows the spars and spar webbing in place. Note that the bellcrank mounting plate has small ply reinforcing plates glued to the ribs.

tubing (Fig. 9.7). Use a scrap of wood, cut to length, to ensure that the tube cuts the holes at exactly the same height on each rib. Glue the snake and the bellcrank in place, and *then* plank the LE and TE, holding them in place while drying with the other board, as before. Add the cap strips.

With a modelling knife, cut back the blue foam supports about ½in. so that you can sand the LE of the panel while it is still stuck in place on the board. Do this with the longest sanding block you can manage. When the edges of the planking and the ribs are nicely flush, you can add the LE spar. (If you want a really strong, lightweight job, cut a strip of 2–3oz glass cloth, put it on the spar with epoxy resin – or glue – and fit the spar so that the cloth is against the planking and ribs.) Razor-plane and sand the LE as far as possible, while the panel is still attached to the building board, then carefully break it free and finish the top side of the LE.

You now have a very strong, extremely rigid and warp-free wing panel. The ailerons are cut in the usual way, and faced with balsa of suitable thickness – ¼in. is a good size, for this allows the hinge a good purchase. Alternatively, add balsa blocks (Fig. 9.8).

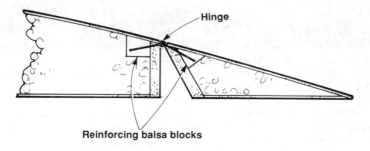

Reinforcing balsa blocks

Fig. 9.8 Reinforcing for aileron hinges

Thin ply plate reinforcement

To aileron

Bellcrank support

The same type of reinforcement
is used for U/C blocks etc.

Blue foam blanks
showing lower surface cut

Fig. 9.9 Ply reinforcement of blue foam ribs

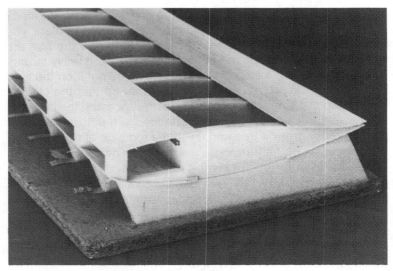

Here the edges of the blanks have been undercut to make it possible to sand the leading and trailing edge with the panel still *in situ* on the cradle. Warping is practically impossible.

When the second panel has been made – beware of the syndrome! – sand the root panels to the angle corresponding to the dihedral required, fit the dihedral brace and epoxy glue the two together. All that remains to be done is to fit the wing tips and your wing is complete.

A finished Laser panel – extremely light, but more than strong enough.

Of course, within the method given here you can make all sorts of modifications, such as slots for undercarriage fixing blocks on low-wing models. In this case, it is as well to use thin plywood doublers on one side of each of the foam ribs, around the slots, to spread landing loads (Fig. 9.9). Even blue foam has its limits! The whole wing can be sheeted, but this would defeat the object of the exercise, without adding significant strength. Flaps can be fitted, as can strut anchor points. It is all a matter of doing things at the appropriate moment. Indeed, experience shows that a check list is most useful, since if a step is forgotten, it is sometimes very difficult to back-track.

Check list
1. Mark out building board.
2. Glue blanks in place, at 90 degrees to board.
3. Fit upper templates.
4. Spot glue top board on blanks.
5. HWC for upper surface.
6. Fit upper surface spar.
7. Fit LE and TE planking, using second board.
8. Fit cap strips.
9. Spot glue upper board on blank edges.
10. Fit templates and cut lower surface.
11. Turn over, cut spar slots.
12. Cut and fit webbing and spar.
13. IMPORTANT! Stop and think about control runs, servo boxes, undercarriage blocks, flaps, dihedral braces and any other fittings which cannot be done later.
14. Fit LE and TE planking, using second board.

15. Fit cap strips.
16. Sand LE and fit LE spar.
17. Unstick panel, and finish.

If you follow this check list carefully, there is very little chance of anything going wrong.

10 JOINING WING PANELS

Categories

We have now seen several methods of making wings using foam, but one thing is common to all; we have hardly mentioned joining them together. In order to simplify the matter, we can immediately separate into two categories one-piece wings, up to about 72in. span, and the larger type, mainly for gliders, which are normally kept in two pieces, mainly to make it easier to transport them. In fact, the arbitrary 72in. limit is largely a rule of thumb, because it is a size that will go into most family cars without too much difficulty, and, of course, it suits the traditional 36in. wood lengths.

Let us now take a look at individual cases, starting with our famous 50in. Clark Y sectioned trainer wing. And straight away, we find ourselves on dangerous ground, because there are two distinct schools of thought on the subject.

Dihedral braces

The classic method is to use a dihedral brace. This is a small piece of plywood, 2–3mm thick, depending on the size of the wing, which is slotted into grooves in the roots of the two panels, usually at the point of maximum thickness on the chord width, and glued firmly in place. This brace is cut in a shallow 'V' shape to suit the desired angle between the two panels (Fig. 10.1).

Should this brace be fitted under the wing skins, or flush with them? Personal logic tells me that it should go under the skins, so that it is glued to them, thus preserving the structural integrity of the two panels. Some modellers, however, advocate skinning the

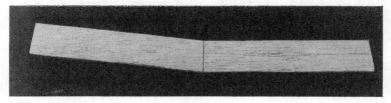

A simple 3mm plywood dihedral brace.

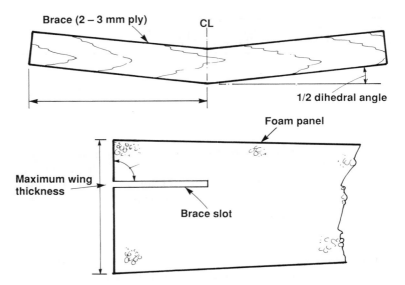

Brace (2 – 3 mm ply)

CL

1/2 dihedral angle

Foam panel

Maximum wing thickness

Brace slot

Fig. 10.1 Ordinary dihedral brace

wing first, then cutting the slots, and gluing the brace in place, finally sanding it down flush with the skins. Both methods are used by individuals and manufacturers, so you can take your choice. If you decide to fit the brace under the skins, you will have to cut slots in the foam cores before the skinning process. Having decided on the length of the brace – generally, the slot will be between one-eighth and one-sixth of the semi-span – mark its position very accurately on the top of the core. The line *must* be exactly at right-angles to the finished root, or gaps will appear at the join, and the angle will be incorrect (Fig. 10.2). There are several ways to cut the slot. It is not worthwhile making HWC templates for this job; it is easier, and faster, with a metal ruler and a long,

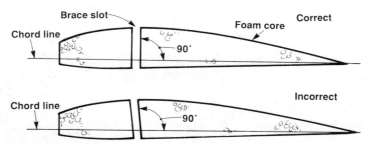

Brace slot

Foam core   Correct

Chord line

90°

Incorrect

Chord line

90°

Fig. 10.2 Vertical slot walls

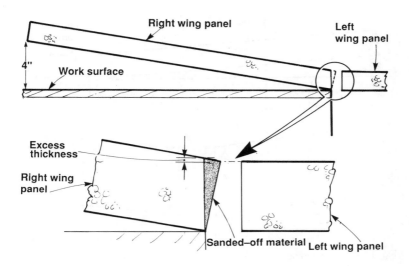

Fig. 10.3 Root sanding – incorrect

sharp blade. An alternative is to tape several hacksaw blades together, until you obtain a width slightly less than that of the brace. The important point, when cutting the slot, is to get the walls absolutely vertical. If you fail to do this, one panel will be at a slight angle to the other, effectively warping the wing, and your model will never fly correctly.

Once the slot has been cut out, use some very fine sandpaper, backed with a thin piece of wood, to true up the walls, and to bring them back to vertical if they are slightly out. You should aim at opening the slot until the brace will just slide in without too much pressure. Don't forget that it will be covered with glue when you come to the final fitting.

The panels are skinned in the usual way, and eventually they are ready for joining. Here you must avoid that short-cut tried by so many modellers, which inevitably leads, not to disaster, but to an unsightly wing joint. Let us suppose that our 50in. wing requires one tip to be propped up 4in. for correct dihedral. The beginner's tendency is to take one panel, pack the tip up 4in, and sand the root vertical (Fig. 10.3). This is quite wrong! If you only sand one root at an angle, you will automatically increase the apparent thickness of the chord, and when this is offered up to the unsanded root, they are no longer the same thickness. The solution, of course, is to block each panel up in turn by 2in, and sand each root (Fig. 10.4). This way, they will both increase in

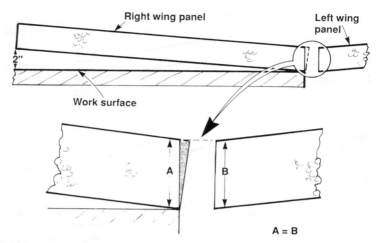

Fig. 10.4 Root sanding – correct

thickness by the same amount, and will match when fitted together. As far as sanding is concerned, use small, circular movements, and keep the sanding block as vertical as possible – a good tip is to clamp one of the set-squares used for sizing the foam blocks to the work-surface, a little way from the panel, and then sight along the sanding board and the vertical edge.

When you have finished, slide the dihedral brace into one slot, make any adjustments necessary by sanding, then slide the other panel into place, and again adjust, until you have a perfect fit. To glue the whole thing together, slow-setting epoxy glue is best, though PVA can be used. Put a piece of plastic on the work surface, to avoid gluing the wing to it, smear all the parts,

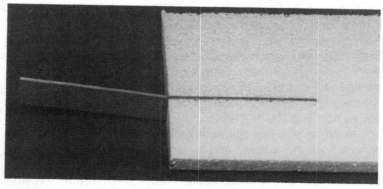

The dihedral brace is check-fitted.

including the panel roots, with epoxy, and fit together. Place the assembled wing on the table, and chock up the tips the required amount. Once more, be careful. If the panels are twisted, it means problems. Cut two special blocks for packing, making sure that the sides are perfectly parallel. Now, if the joint line and the flat undersurface of each panel is firmly in contact with the work surface and the blocks respectively, the panels must be at the same angle. Check this. If there is any misalignment, it is quite possible to correct it by using some weights on the panels, to hold them in place. Make sure that the glue is completely dry before attempting to move the wing.

The wing is now in one piece, and, after covering, is ready for use. However, as you will see in the next section, we can strengthen this joint, though whether it is necessary is open to debate.

Bandage joints

The second type of wing joint does not need a dihedral brace, though one can be added if you think it is necessary; many modellers do. My own opinion is that it is a case of overkill, or overbuilding, if you prefer, which adds only unnecessary weight. Experience shows that if the wing is to break, it will not be at the joint (provided the joint has been properly made) but elsewhere along the span. What, then, is the point in reinforcing a joint which is already more than strong enough? Enough preaching; back to work. Sand the two panel roots, as previously described, set the panels up with their packing, and check. Adjust, if necessary, and when they are perfectly matched, smear the roots with epoxy, and then glue them together.

To reinforce this joint, you will need some 1–2oz glass cloth, and a little resin, either epoxy or polyester, or epoxy glue. In the case of a small wing, you can even use medical bandage or a piece of nylon stocking material, with PVA as the adhesive. Measure the width of the fuselage at the wing-seat, add ½in. to this figure, and measure off half this distance on each side of the wing-joint. Brush on a coating of resin or glue on the upper surface between these two marks, cut a piece of the chosen material to the same width, and lay it carefully on the joint. It should run from the TE to just around the LE (Fig. 10.5). Don't try to cover both sides of the wing with one piece of cloth, especially if there is a lot of dihedral, or you will get a series of rucks in it. Thoroughly wet the cloth with the resin. If you are going to use epoxy glue, you will find that it is too thick to wet the tissue – don't worry, borrow the family's

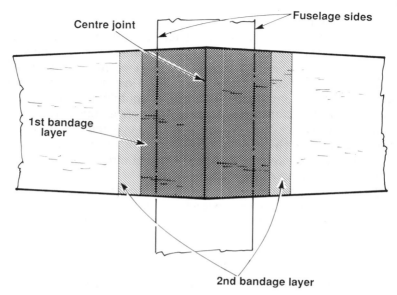

Centre joint — Fuselage sides

1st bandage layer

2nd bandage layer

Fig. 10.5 Bandage joint

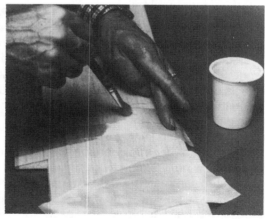

The first layer of glass-cloth is being covered with resin. You can see the wetting effect of the section already done. The second layer is lying on the wing, ready for use.

electric hairdryer, or use your heat gun, and the glue will quickly become liquid enough. With PVA glue, it may be necessary to dilute it a little with water.

Cut a second piece of cloth, about two inches wider than the first, and lay this on top, wetting it thoroughly again. Get as smooth a surface as you can with the brush, and leave it to dry. Turn the wing over, remove any resin or glue which has run, and repeat the operation on the underside, making sure you overlap the tissue at the leading edge.

When everything is quite dry, the last job is to rub down the bandage, using wet-and-dry paper. Some care is required not to spoil the surface adjacent to the joint, especially if the skin is balsa. To avoid this, place some wide sticky tape on the skin, butting up against the edge of the bandage. This will protect the wing skin. When the joint is nice and smooth, the job is finished.

Why use two layers of cloth? In the first place, two thin laminations are stronger than one thick one, and secondly the extra inch you have allowed on each side of the second lamination will spread the load more evenly. There is nothing worse than a sudden transition from a strong section to a weaker one – this is where breakage will always occur.

Laser method wings

This type of wing is somewhat more complicated in construction than the plain foam core wing, so provision should be made at the planning stage for the slots to take a dihedral brace. Alternatively, the wing roots can be fully sheeted out as far as the third rib in each panel, and the bandage system can be used; or even both methods together. In the case of a high-wing model, bandage plus flying struts are quite sufficient. On a low-wing model, the undercarriage block can be cut in one piece, thus doubling as a brace.

Brown paper wings

My preference here is for a bandage, in order to reinforce the wing where the elastic bands used to fix it to the fuselage exert some pressure on the skin. A dihedral brace is quite in order to add strength, not to the joint but the wing panels themselves. It is a good idea to cut a longer dihedral brace than usual – perhaps a little over a quarter of the semi-span – and then taper it as shown in Fig. 10.6 in order to avoid that weak transition point. PVA glue can be used in this case.

CL   2 – 3 mm ply brace

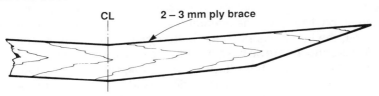

Fig. 10.6 Tapered dihedral brace

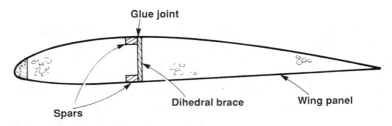

Fig. 10.7 Gluing spars and dihedral brace

Delta wings

Here again, either of the two main methods of panel joining can be used, but in this case the joint made by gluing the two roots together will, in itself, constitute quite a strong joint, first because of the relatively large gluing surface at the root ribs of the delta planform, and secondly because the smaller span of delta models relative to their conventional counterparts, for a given engine size, will impose less load on the joint. A thin bandage should be sufficient in this case.

Unskinned blue foam wings

Because these wings have no skin the bandage method is not appropriate, especially as it would cause local thickening which would show up under the iron-on film. Thus, the dihedral brace is best. If there are no spars used, then a brace tapered in depth (see Fig. 10.6 again) should be used in order to spread load stresses. If spars are incorporated in the structure, then an ordinary brace can be used (Fig. 10.7). Make sure that it is glued firmly to the spars themselves, as shown, as indeed it should be whenever it is used in a wing with spars.

Two-piece glider wings

So far we have been dealing with panels which are joined to each other. In this section we look at panels which are plugged into the fuselage. Here again, the variety of methods of joining is quite wide; dural tongues, ply tongues, round joiners, flat strip joiners, and so on. However, the general principle is the same in all these cases, the variations needed being a matter of common sense. We will concentrate on the flat steel strip type of joiner which slides into a dural or brass box fitted inside the fuselage – a system which is becoming more and more widely used, particularly on large models. Again, there are two methods; in the first, short joiners which meet in the centre of the box are fitted to each wing panel

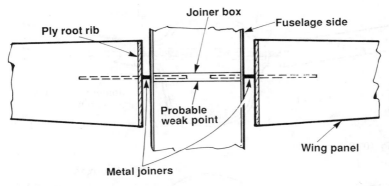

Fig. 10.8 Single joiner box

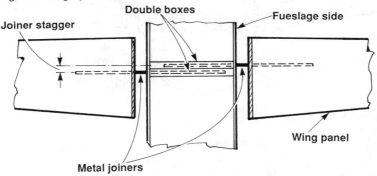

Fig. 10.9 Double joiner boxes

(Fig. 10.8); in the second, long joiners are used, fitting into individual boxes which are glued together (Fig. 10.9). The choice depends on the individual; but the second method is probably stronger. I have seen several models using the first method that have had the joiners break their box at the point where they meet. The answer, of course, is to avoid heavy landings – not always possible!

Whether you use a tongue, round or flat joiners, the principle is the same; in the first type you have to calculate very accurately the angle of the joiner in the wing, to obtain the correct dihedral, and in the second, the joiner is parallel with the upper surface of the wing, which is finished before fitting the boxes in the fuselage (Fig. 10.10). In this latter case, there will be a slight fore and aft stagger in the position of the joiners in the two panels, but you can glue the boxes in place using the wings themselves for accurate alignment (Fig. 10.11).

Whichever system you use, the basic problem is how to firmly

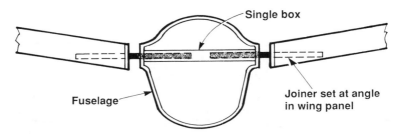

Fig. 10.10 Single box

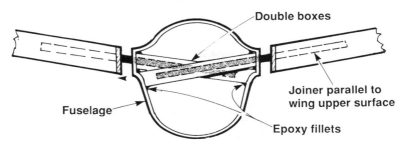

Fig. 10.11 Double box

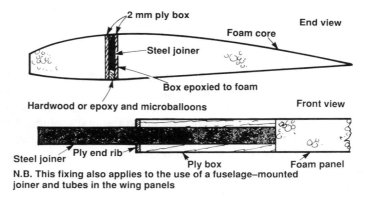

Fig. 10.12 Joiner wing fixing (double box system)

attach metal joiners in the wing-panel roots. The generally-accepted practice is to build-up a plywood box around the joiner, whether it be flat or round, using slow-setting epoxy glue (Fig. 10.12). 2 or 3mm plywood of fairly good quality is necessary, and the final height of the box thus constructed should be the same as the thickness of the foam core where it is attached. It can be made very slightly oversize, and then sanded down to suit.

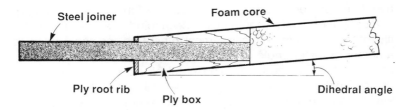

Fig. 10.13 Joiner wing fixing (single box system)

Let's take the short joiners first. In this case they will not be parallel to the upper surface of the wing, but at a slight angle to it; this angle dictating the dihedral of the finished model. Once you know this angle – let us say 3 degrees – all you have to do is make the two sides of the ply box, and then cut the top and bottom edges of this box at an angle of 3 degrees (Fig. 10.13). Fit the metal joiner with plenty of epoxy glue – this is one area where you don't worry too much about weight; strength is more important – and clamp the whole thing together.

While it is drying, cut slots in the appropriate place in the two cores. These slots must be at right-angles to the root, and very slightly larger than the dimensions of the joiner boxes, to allow for the epoxy coating. When all is ready, make a trial fitting without glue, to make sure that they are sitting square in the slots. When satisfied, glue in place.

Long joiners are slightly easier to arrange because you need not worry about the dihedral angle; the joiners must be perfectly parallel with the upper surface of the wing panel. However, one joiner slot must be slightly ahead of the other, to compensate for the fact that one box in the fuselage is glued in front of the other. Otherwise, the operation is the same. Follow an identical pro-cedure if you intend to use fairly large-diameter dural tubes, as on some high-performance sailplanes, but don't forget to seal the ends of the tubes temporarily, to avoid glue getting into them.

Once the joiners have been epoxied into the foam cores, you can go ahead and skin them in the usual way, but do make sure that the boxes are flush with the surfaces of the cores, otherwise they will cause unsightly bumps on the finished surface. In the case of long wing panels skinned with obechi and balsa skins you may add a small triangle of glass cloth over the end of the panel, in addition to the full-length triangle, to strengthen the joiner area. If you do this on a GRP wing, it is better to use two triangles, of thinner cloth, one quite a bit bigger than the other. This is again to avoid bumps due to different thicknesses of the surface covering.

A couple of points should be borne in mind: make sure that the flat metal joiners are perfectly vertical, otherwise one panel will be at a higher or lower angle of incidence than the other, which is the equivalent of a warped wing. The metal joiners should be perfectly centred in the ply boxes, or your model will exhibit the 'one-wing-low' syndrome, which is unsightly. Whichever system you use, the panel is finished by sticking a rib of good-quality plywood, 3 or 4mm thick, to the root of the panel and sanding it to blend with the surfaces. Use epoxy glue. This rib is there to avoid any crushing of the panel when the wings move forward and back-wards slightly on landing, due to their inertia. (Incidentally, fit cross-pieces in the fuselage where the leading and trailing edges of the panels touch it, to avoid the same damage to the fuselage.) This rib also strengthens the joint between the joiner box and the foam panel.

So far I have advocated joiners being glued into the wings, which is probably the most logical choice, especially when transport is taken into consideration. It is just as possible, of course, to glue the tubes or boxes into the wing-roots, and have the joiners glued into the fuselage. Mechanically there is little difference, but joiners sticking out of the sides do make transport of larger fuselages more difficult.

11 FUSELAGES

The full-size world

Although many enthusiasts may not realise it, the use of foam in the construction of fuselages is almost as wide a subject as that of its use in wings. It ranges from the making of simple parts of the fuselage, such as turtledecks, right up to the totally foam construction. It is interesting to speculate on which came first, the chicken or the egg, or, in this case, foam models or full-size foam aircraft? The question is a valid one, since there are now quite a few amateur full-size planes around, such as the VariEze, the Quickie and even the famous Voyager, all made of shaped foam and GRP. There is even the case of Cliff Weirick, a well-known American R/C modeller, who built his own half-scale Corsair from these materials; equipped complete with a 115hp Lycoming engine, it is capable of 150mph! Where do we draw the line between models and full-size planes, particularly when their construction is identical?

Turtledeck construction

What does matter is that there are ways of using foam in fuselage construction that are tried and tested, but not widely known about. Let us start with making parts of fuselages. The one that leaps to mind straight away is the turtledeck – the top of the fuselage behind the cockpit (Fig. 11.1). One of the reasons so many

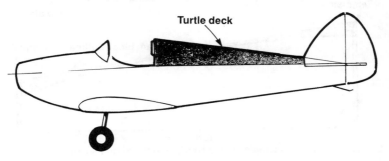

Turtle deck

Fig. 11.1 Turtle deck

modellers and manufacturers turn to foam for this is that it is fairly easy to cut with a HWC, since it is basically a long, thin half-cone. The upper surface may be straight or slightly curved, but it can still be cut with the wire.

The first thing is to decide whether to use white or blue foam. If the lines are almost straight, with just very slight curves, white foam will do, because there will be very little sanding. If, on the other hand, the curve is pronounced, blue foam may be more useful, since it is so much easier to sand than the white variety. Whichever is chosen, the technique is the same.

From your plan, decide on the overall dimensions of the turtledeck to be made, and then size up a block of the appropriate foam in the same way as a wing block. It should be about ½in. oversize all round.

Next, make up a couple of templates for the front and rear ends of the block. Be careful – if the turtledeck is curved, it will be necessary to cut these templates oversize, to allow for the highest point on the piece (Fig. 11.2). Since you will be cutting right down to the bottom of the foam block, put it on a small piece of wood – preferably with a couple of pieces of double-sided tape and put a few weights on top (Fig. 11.3).

Cutting the turtledeck with the HWC follows exactly the same process as the cutting of a wing core, except for one thing. Given that the wire will have to travel vertically at the beginning and the

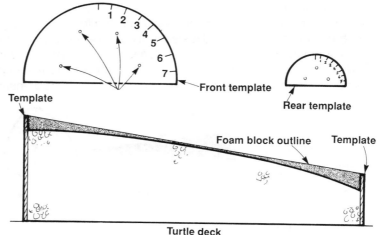

Turtle deck
Cut basic shape with templates and HWC, sand down to final shape

Fig. 11.2 Turtle deck formers and pronounced curve turtle deck

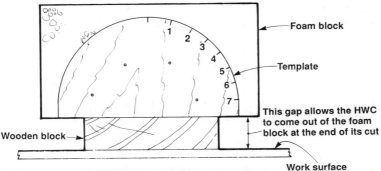

Fig. 11.3 Mounting foam block to cut turtle deck

end of the cut, there is no way that you can use an electric drive unit on the HWC. Like it or not, you are going to have to recruit someone to hold the other end!

Once the cut has been made, any necessary sanding should be carried out, taking care to test fit the part in place frequently, to check just how much more you have to remove. Remember, it is easy to sand off material, it is quite another matter to put some back on if you go too far – in fact, with foam, it is practically impossible, so check! If you are using white foam, you will almost certainly need to skin the component, so make allowance for the thickness of the skin you are going to use. In the case of blue foam, it is quite possible to leave it without a true skin, and just cover it with heat-shrink film, or fabric.

On some models, such as those with electric power, low weight is extremely important, so it may be necessary to reduce the weight of the turtledeck as far as possible. If it is essentially straight-tapered this is easy – just cut out the centre of the templates, as shown, put the part back in its off-cut, weight it, and scoop out the interior with the HWC (Fig. 11.4). The weight saving may not seem very great, but when you are trying to eliminate every gram, it counts, especially if you follow the same principle throughout the structure. An alternative method is to use pins (Fig. 11.5).

It is up to the individual modeller to decide where the technique is applicable on any specific model, although, as we shall see later, it forms the basis of another technique.

Profiling

The next process to discuss is profiling. As the word implies, this means that foam is used to achieve the final outline of a model. It

Fig. 11.4 Hollow templates

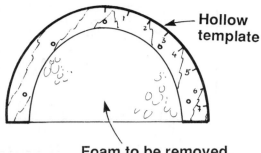

Hollow template

Foam to be removed

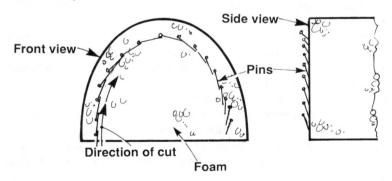

A turtle-deck cut with templates and the HWC. The cockpit was also cut in the same way.

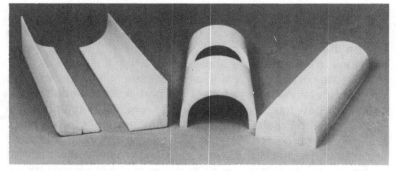

Side view

Front view

Pins

Direction of cut

Foam

Fig. 11.5 Alternative method

is particularly useful on fuselages which are full of curves, and it is an excellent way of making models which would otherwise require a quite high degree of skill in planking. That does not mean that no skill is needed, but a difficult job becomes easier, and thus within the reach of more modellers.

An alternative method of cutting out the centre to reduce weight. The HWC is simply run round the line formed by ordinary dress-making pins, instead of cutting out a special template.

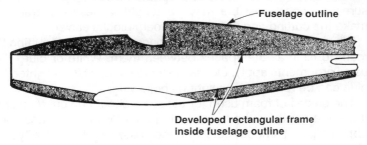

Fuselage outline

Developed rectangular frame inside fuselage outline

Fig. 11.6 Basic wooden frame inside fuselage outline

Within the outline of any fuselage with a lot of curves, it is possible to draw a small, squared-off frame in side and plan view (Fig. 11.6). This means that it is possible to make a basic structure of balsa sheet or spruce and balsa strip which will be big enough to hold the radio gear and the engine bulkhead, and will provide fixing points for the wings, rudder and tailplane. Think about it: the resulting aircraft, if left in this state, would resemble that most famous model in the USA, the Ugly Stick. Well-named, too, which is why we have more work to do! It is possible, using foam sheeting stuck to the outside of this basic frame, to build up the fuselage, and then sand it down to the shape of the plane you want.

One method is to cut up sheets of foam of the size necessary, fix them to the frame, and then sand to shape, in the same way that you would a model built from thick balsa sheet. However, the sanding process will require a lot of eyeballing and templates to get it just right, and is a rather fastidious job. There is a better way.

Go back to the plan, and draw on it the basic frame that you

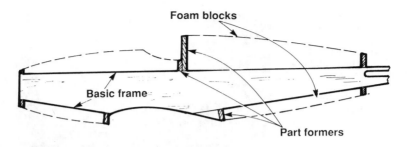

Foam blocks

Basic frame

Part formers

Fig. 11.7 Adding formers to basic frame

have made, being very careful to use the outside dimensions. This will allow you to draw small formers which can be fixed to the outside of the frame in the appropriate places (Fig. 11.7). Make sure that, where possible, they are at right-angles to the frame, to make the cutting and fitting of the foam blocks easier.

When all the part-formers are in place, you can start cutting the foam to fill in all the spaces between them. White or blue? The usual arguments apply, blue is easier to sand, white is lighter, but blue can be reduced in weight by hollowing.

The pieces of foam used for the sides should be cut to exactly the same depth as the frame, using the HWC where possible to obtain square, smooth cuts, and then glued in place. The type of glue used is not important, except that if white PVA is used, be prepared to wait some time – a couple of days or more – for it to dry, since the foam prevents air getting to it. Whatever glue is used, there is a golden rule in this type of construction. Never apply glue in places where you are going to sand, because the glue line thus created will have a different density to the rest of the foam, will not sand in the same way, and will make it practically impossible to obtain a smooth surface. Glue the blocks to the frame only.

When the side blocks are in place, cut the blocks that go across the fuselage horizontally: these will sit both on the frame itself and on the flat surfaces of the vertical blocks (Fig. 11.8). The result will be an oversized block of foam, made up from a series of smaller blocks, and will not look anything like the plane you want. Don't worry, it soon will.

If you are using blue foam, and you want to reduce weight as much as possible, you will have to spot-glue the blocks in place, shape the fuselage until it is approximately the right shape but still a little oversize, then remove each block and hollow it out. Stick them back in place, permanently this time, and finish the shaping.

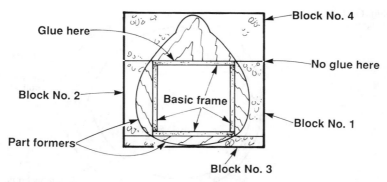

Fig. 11.8 Front view of foam-block clad basic frame

The resulting fuselage will be very light.

As far as the actual shaping is concerned, choose your favourite weapon. Mine is a long-bladed cutter with a new blade. If this is used with a slicing movement, it is an excellent method of removing the excess foam. I have also used an electric carving knife to good effect, but care must be taken not to use too much pressure; let the blades do the cutting at their own speed. One useful trick is to take off the excess corners with the HWC, using the set-squares for sizing blocks as guides, the fuselage being chocked up, or held by another person, between them. Another, perhaps more flexible method, is to use pieces of piano-wire or thin bamboo kebab skewers, stuck through the foam at strategic points and used as guides (Fig. 11.9).

Remember, if you cut it off, you can't stick it back on, so carve

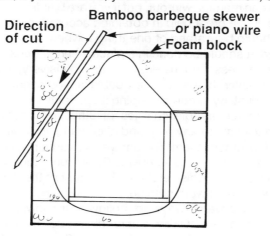

Fig. 11.9 Removing excess foam with HWC

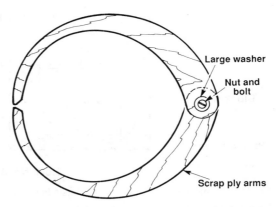

Fig. 11.10 Home-made calipers

Large washer

Nut and bolt

Scrap ply arms

down to the general outline, still keeping oversize. Having got this far, out with the sanding blocks. These need to be fairly long, and you will need a variety of grades, coarse for the initial work, going right down to 600 grade wet-and-dry paper, used dry, for the final finish. Use your ingenuity for areas like the inside curves on wing fillets. Varying diameters of dowelling, broom handles, fish-paste bottle – you name it, all can be used to obtain the exact shape you need. Use light strokes, otherwise you will dig bits out of the foam. Make sure that there are no folds in the sandpaper, for these will dig in and tear the foam. Beware too of the edges of the sanding blocks or the paper itself, all potential foam diggers.

One useful tool that you can make up is an outsized caliper, as shown in Fig 11.10, made from scrap wood. If you have a good eye, you can manage without, but if you are building a scale model fuselage, it is a great help in obtaining accurate dimensions.

You should be warned of one thing – when white or blue foam is sanded, it should be done in a place where it does not matter if you make a mess. The material you take off is very, very fine, and it will fly all over the place. The trouble is, you cannot get rid of it like balsa dust, by simply sweeping it up. Foam dust and particles accumulate remarkable charges of static electricity and stick quite tenaciously to anything and everything, including the brush intended to remove them! The answer is a vacuum cleaner. In fact, during the winter, I sand alongside the vacuum tube which I fix in the Workmate, and this catches 75 per cent of the dust as I sand. In good weather, I work outside.

There are several ways to hollow out individual blocks – necessary if you are building a very light model. First, mark out the area you want to eliminate with a felt pen. Then you can dig away

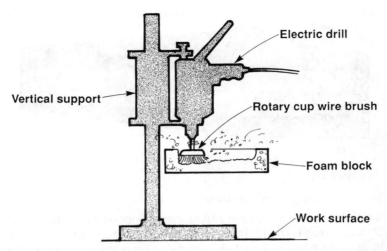

Fig. 11.11 Hollowing foam blocks using rotary wire brush

with a modelling knife, or a small drill-bit in one of those little 12v electric drills. But the method I find most efficient is one I first saw advocated by Dave Chinnery in RCM&E. A small cup-shaped wire brush is put in the chuck of an ordinary electric drill, and the latter is fixed in some way – I use a vertical support. The drill is set in motion, and the block is then presented to the brush, which will then scrub off the foam (Fig. 11.11). If you hold the outer surface in your hand you will be able to feel when the brush is down to within 5–7mm of it, and that is the time to stop! Practise on some scrap first; it is not difficult, but needs a little getting used to.

A modification of this method is to use a router in the drill, and to use the vertical press to set the height of the cut. The block is then moved around on the press table until you have removed all the excess material. Both are easier to do than to explain.

As you can see, this method of using foam to fill out and then carve down a fuselage can be very flexible. It also gives a very strong airframe – the Ryan PT-22 on the cover has a 6 × 6mm lattice-work spruce frame covered with blue foam, and a 3oz glass cloth skin. The engine is a converted chain-saw job of 44cc, span is 2.5m, and it is stronger than it need be, whilst weighing just 10kg. Incidentally, the wings are made by the Laser method, which also contributes to the light weight.

Foam throughout
Yet another method of making fuselages is to use foam practically

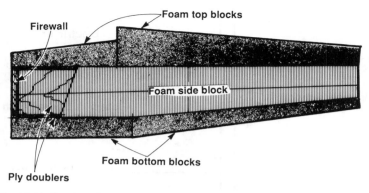

Firewall, Foam top blocks, Foam side block, Foam bottom blocks, Ply doublers

Fig. 11.12 Fuselage from foam blocks

throughout, and in this case blue foam is necessary. White is not strong enough. The range of models that can be made in this way is vast, from small, 7-cell electric pylon racers right up to a 3.2m Curtiss P-6E fitted with a 75cc petrol engine. The only wood is used for the firewall and small doublers in the case of models with large engines, and the balsa reinforcement in such things as wings and tailplanes and fins.

The system is very similar to the previous one, starting with drawing a central box on the plan. In this case, however, there is no frame as such. The lines of the box indicate the inner faces of the sheets of foam used to form the fuselage (Fig. 11.12). These are cut out, and the two sides are then glued to the top deck. Formers are added, followed by the firewall and its supporting doublers, and the bottom sheet is then glued in place. Once again, it is most important to plan the gluing in such a way that you will never be required to sand across a glue line.

The actual shaping starts by transferring fuselage outlines from the plan to the foam blocks. Take off as much material as possible using the HWC and then start the more delicate work with blade and sanding block. This time you will not have the part-formers to help you, so you will have to rely on your eyes, the caliper, and outside templates, cut from stiff card.

To produce lightweight fuselages in this way, it is necessary to assemble the sides dry, mark the former positions on the insides, and then rout out the foam in between the former positions (Fig. 11.13). As far as the formers are concerned, two layers of laminated balsa, with the grain running in opposite directions, are sufficient on all but the very largest planes. You can go even further and make the formers from foam and GRP. It is easy and light. Cut

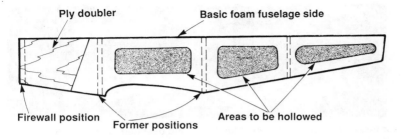

Fig. 11.13 Marking foam fuselage sides

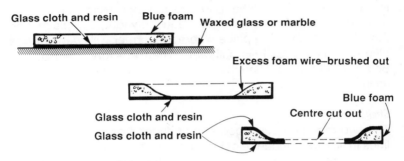

Fig. 11.14 Blue foam GRP formers

the former from 6–10mm thick blue foam, depending on the size of the model, and cover one side of it with 3oz glass cloth and resin. I place mine on a flat piece of marble (once a mantel-shelf) well polished with a non-silicone polish. When it is set, the majority of the foam is routed out, leaving sloping edges, and the other side is then glassed (Fig. 11.14). Finally the centre is cut out, leaving an extremely strong 'picture-frame' former, which weighs very little.

On the large models – for 15cc engines and upwards, and the larger gliders – a fuselage built of foam skinned on the outside will not really be strong enough. The solution is to skin both sides, inside and out. Glass cloth is probably the best choice, but is not to everyone's taste. Obechi, or other veneers can be used, as can balsa (which is expensive) and brown paper. Glass cloth will give the best results on the really big models, such as quarter-scale craft, where a layer of 4oz cloth on each side has been shown to be sufficient. One point bears mentioning. If you hollow out the fuselage sides and then skin the interior, the GRP will be set when you come to epoxy the formers into place. Now, it is a fact that epoxy resin – or glue – does not stick well to a smooth epoxy surface. It is thus necessary to have a rough surface where the

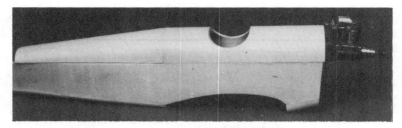

A fuselage made solely from blue foam, and destined for a Laser 61 FS. The decks are not yet permanent fixtures, and require some sanding, especially at the rear of the fuselage.

former, or indeed any other part, has to be glued in place. To do this, cut a strip of Solartex of the required width, and place it on the GRP surface at the place where the former will eventually be glued, while the GRP is still wet. When it is dry, peel off the Solartex, and you will find that it has left a rough area, ideal for the resin to key into.

Straight line specials

The two methods described above depend on drawing straight lines inside the silhouette of the fuselage, and are perfectly viable ways of building. Another technique depends on being able to draw straight lines, this time on the *outside* of the silhouette! Quite a few aircraft are based on straight lines which have been rounded off to obtain the required shape. The classic example is the Swiss Pilatus B4 aerobatic glider, developed in Germany in 1966 and built under licence in Switzerland from 1972. Since the fuselage was made mainly from aluminium sheet, it was designed as a series of cones, with the exception of the nose, of course (Fig. 11.15). It is really quite simple to produce the fuselage by reducing

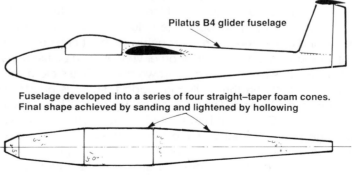

Pilatus B4 glider fuselage

Fuselage developed into a series of four straight–taper foam cones. Final shape achieved by sanding and lightened by hollowing

Fig. 11.15 Fuselage based on straight lines

The templates are adjusted so that the cones, in their off–cuts on a flat surface, are perfectly aligned

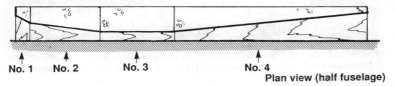

No. 1   No. 2   No. 3   No. 4

Plan view (half fuselage)

Fig. 11.16 Cutting cones for Pilatus B4

Note: Keel and foam blocks are hollowed to make room for R/C gear, and to lighten

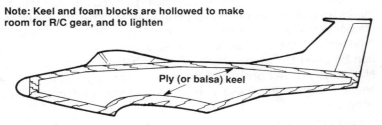

Ply (or balsa) keel

Fig. 11.17 Ply keel system

it to a number of half cones on the side view. These are then cut from foam, using templates and the same method as that used to produce turtledecks, and then assembled, first to make a half-fuselage longitudinally, and then by glueing the two halves together (Fig. 11.16). On smaller models the fuselage is skinned on the outside; on larger ones a double skin is used. This method is a favourite one with the PSS specialists (Power Slope Soarers) since it is possible to make very light models in this way.

In some cases it is possible to reduce the silhouette to straight lines in certain places, and not in others. Here, a mixture of methods can be used. The easiest is to use a keel (Fig. 11.17). This is a thin plywood or balsa outline of the fuselage side. The interior is cut out to suit the thickness of the foam sections used. These sections are then cut out and lined up on the keel, having made allowance for the thickness of the latter. The parts that cannot be developed as straight lines are then cut out as blocks, shaped very roughly, and then added to the rest. Using the more accurately cut pieces, it is then a relatively simple matter to cut and sand these parts down to blend into the general line of the fuselage. If necessary, part-formers can also be used to help in the shaping process.

Of course, the permutations are practically infinite. You can combine all sorts of methods, according to the fuselage to be

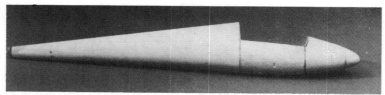

A fuselage made up on a keel – the part-formers can be seen between the foam blocks.

made. Indeed, as you get into the matter, you will almost certainly find yourself inventing new ways of doing things. For example, the cutting of hollowed-out cone sections can be done in two phases; an inside cut, and then an outside one. Dave Chinnery found this a rather slow process, so he invented a sort of foam 'lathe' which can be used to cut any angle of cone, hollowed out, in one go. Naturally, this will only work if the cone has a perfectly circular section, but in this case it is a very useful, and cheap, little accessory.

One criticism of foam fuselages, especially where early scale models are concerned, is that it looks wrong. There is a relatively simple way of getting around this. Many aircraft of the period had stringered fuselages, and, with a little bit of cheating, it is quite easy to give our foam fuselage a similar appearance. Thin stringers of hard balsa, pine, spruce or even small-diameter dowel, are glued onto the surface of the fuselage, and the whole thing is then covered (Fig. 11.10). The results looks very much like a built-up structure, providing, of course, that the covering is sufficiently opaque. An added advantage of this method is that the stringers will not sag, as they may do on 'real' built-up surfaces due to the shrinking action of the covering. In this case, the stringers are

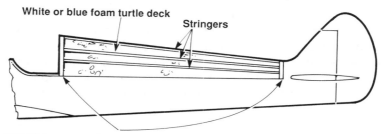

White or blue foam turtle deck

Stringers

N.B. Stringers can have square, triangular or round
sections. They lay flush on the foam surface

Fig. 11.18 Stringers on foam

supported throughout their length by the fuselage surface, and therefore cannot sag.

Foamboard

It would be incorrect, in a book about foam, to leave out a building material which is based on foam, even if it cannot really be put in the same category as the other types.

Foamboard is a sheet of foam, covered on both sides with a thin layer of matt card. It comes in several thicknesses, the most useful being 3mm and 6mm. In weight and price it is comparable with good-quality balsa, and, thanks to its sandwich construction, it is strong. It can be used as a balsa substitute in wings, mainly for ribs. However, its main usefulness lies in fuselage construction.

The disadvantage of foamboard is that it is difficult to build curved surfaces with it, so it is limited to flat, or almost flat, surfaces. Slab-sided fuselages with some curvature in plan view are quite possible. There are also other methods, and more will be developed as the material becomes more popular. However, I have built several fuselages using a specific technique. This, quite simply, involves using square balsa strips at all angles, in order to mask the foam interior of the board, and to reinforce the structure (Fig. 11.19). Epoxy glue is used; the usual precautions about the use of contact glue still apply. However, if it is used only on the card facing, then it will cause no problems.

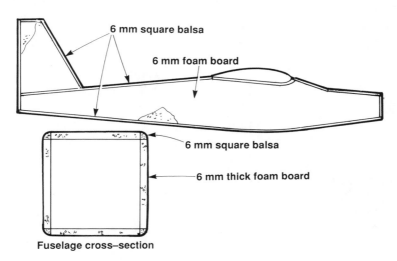

6 mm square balsa

6 mm foam board

6 mm square balsa

6 mm thick foam board

Fuselage cross–section

Fig. 11.19 Use of square balsa strips and foam board

Foamboard, edged with balsa, is also useful for tailplanes and fins. There is structural weakness. One more material to add to the panoply of the perfect foam modeller.

12 OTHER USES

Accessories

So far we have looked at the use of foam as an integral part of the model plane structure, but it must not be forgotten that it can also be used, in a variety of ways, in a secondary role. It can either be used actually to build parts or the patterns used for moulding one-off accessories, as we shall see. One of the most logical uses of the material is in the construction of floats, so we will take a look at this first.

Floats

Foam is a logical material to use for floats, because it is light, and it adds a degree of safety. If a waterplane lands awkwardly, or hits a floating object, there is a possibility of damage. This may result in a dunking and wetting, plus the necessity for repairs before any further flying can take place. With foam, very often a strip of waterproof adhesive tape will provide a temporary repair, and flying can continue.

Relatively little has been printed about float design, but you will need a rule-of-thumb method in order to draw a pair to suit your plane. Figure 12.1 gives general dimensions for sports-type floats that I have used successfully on several models. Whilst most of

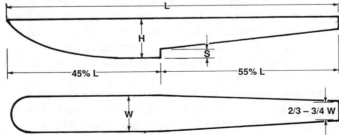

L is 75% – 50% of total fuselage length
W is 10% – 14% of L
S is 10% – 15% of W
H is equal to W

Floats should be fixed about 20% – 25% of wingspan apart
N.B. For very heavy models, err on the generous side

Fig. 12.1 General dimensions for floats

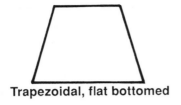

Trapezoidal, flat bottomed

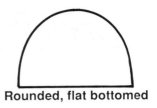

Rounded, flat bottomed

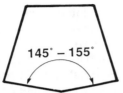

Trapezoidal, V bottomed

Rounded, V bottomed

Fig. 12.2 Float cross-sections

the dimensions are not critical, the centre of gravity should be kept directly above or slightly ahead of the step. The floats should be about a quarter-span apart, and perfectly parallel, with no toe-in. Apart from that, you can make them parallel-sided or tapered, square, trapezoidal or round, with a vertical or raked step, flat or V-bottomed; and you can experiment with the curve on the forward bottom surface. Floats are not super-critical where design is concerned, and most will work (Fig. 12.2).

White or blue foam can be used, but white is lighter, and since they will have a fairly substantial skin, there is no strength problem. The first thing to do is to work out the size of the block you will need in order to make your design. It is more than likely that you will not have a piece of foam thick enough, so you will have to make up a block by sticking two pieces together. Once again, be careful where you spread the glue; remember that cutting or sanding glue lines in foam is difficult to achieve neatly. Work out the outline of the finished floats, and then draw a line inside this silhouette, and spread the glue inside this line (be particularly careful if you are going to make V-bottomed floats!). The block should be about 1in. wider than the finished float (Fig. 12.3).

You will need four templates, one for each end of the float, and two identical ones for the sides. The end plates can be made from thin plywood, as usual, but using this for the side templates would be expensive. This is where you can employ those two sheets of

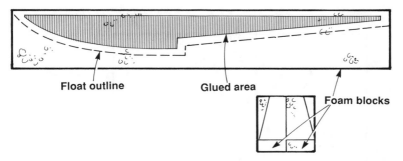

Float outline **Glued area** **Foam blocks**

Fig. 12.3 Glue-line for joining blocks

The foam block on its ply base with template in position, ready for the rounded top part to be cut.

incredibly hard – and heavy – balsawood that you should never have bought!

When the block is cut to size, use double-sided tape to stick it to a piece of wood about ½in. thick and slightly narrower than the minimum width of the finished float – this will allow the wire to exit from the foam at the bottom of the cut when making rounded floats. Pin the two end templates in place, their bottom edges resting on the wooden strip. They should, of course, be numbered in the same way as rib templates, particularly where round floats are concerned. Cut off one side, then the other.

If you are making rounded floats, the numbering should start with 'zero' at the highest point of the template, on the vertical centre-line, and go in both directions (Fig. 12.4). The juncture of the two pieces of foam used to make up the block will probably coincide with this line. Make the first cut by dropping the HWC vertically down from the top of the block to the zero point on the

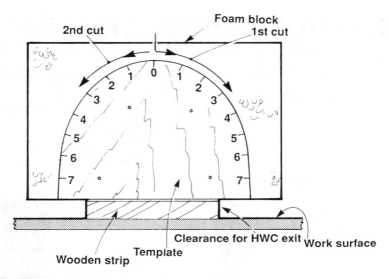

Fig. 12.4 Numbering rounded end templates

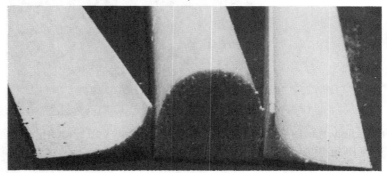

The cut block, with its off-cuts. Note the join in the middle – be careful when cutting past the glue joint.

template, and then cutting around one side. Then replace the HWC at zero, and do the same for the other side.

Whatever the shape of the float, the next job is to put the off-cuts back in place temporarily, using either tacks of glue, or double-sided tape – again, be careful to position them accurately. Turn the block over and fix the side templates in place. We will deal first with flat-bottomed floats. In this case, the templates will be perfectly parallel to each other, and at the same height. When they are in place, pin small pieces of wood vertically at the step position, and use them as guides to drop the HWC down to the

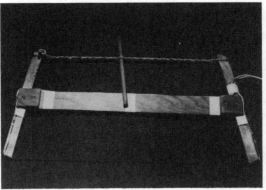

A mini-HWC costs only a few pence and is invaluable when you have to cut small objects by yourself. The cutter is held in one hand, the other being used to steady the work.

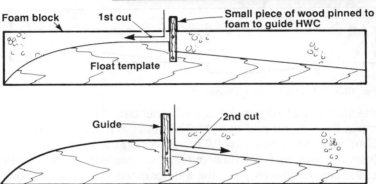

Foam block   1st cut   Small piece of wood pinned to foam to guide HWC

Float template

Guide   2nd cut

Fig. 12.5 Cutting flat-bottomed floats

forward part of the float bottom. Then cut forward to the tip of the bow and bring the HWC out (Fig. 12.5). The second cut then becomes a vertical drop down the face of the step, and back to the end of the float. And that is all there is to it. The foam is ready for skinning.

If you want V-shaped floats, then the process is slightly more complicated. The angle to be aimed for should be about 145–155 degrees. Less, and the lift from the floats will be reduced; more, and you might as well make them flat-bottomed and save yourself the trouble! Draw this angle on the end of the foam, and then place the two templates so that a straight-edge placed over them gives this angle – you will find that generally speaking, one will be about ½in. higher than the edge of the foam, and the other ½in. lower. When you have got them right, fix in place with nails (Fig. 12.6).

This time you will need to make four cuts. The first two are made as before, with the templates in their initial position. Then invert

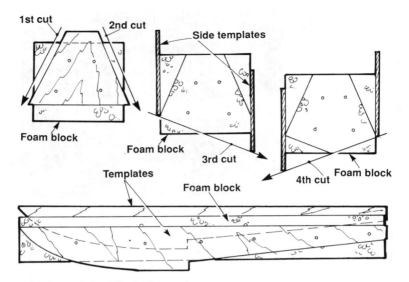

Fig. 12.6 Cutting V-bottomed floats

the positions of the templates, the higher becoming the lower, and make the second pair of cuts. The result is a V-bottomed foam core, with the apex of the 'V' exactly along the centre line of the float. If it isn't, then you have made a mistake with the positioning of the side templates. As usual with foam work, the preparation is very important!

Before skinning the floats, work out the location of the attachment points for the undercarriage (Fig. 12.7). Carefully cut openings in the top of the floats at these points and fit hardwood blocks, using slow-drying epoxy glue. When the glue is dry, very carefully fair these blocks to blend into the general contour of the core – it is best to cut them as close to shape as possible before finally gluing them in place. If the floats are very big, you can set a spar into the top of the float for about three-quarters of the length of the top of the float (Fig. 12.8).

Lastly, skin your floats with balsa, obechi, iron-on film or GRP. Whichever you use, do be careful not to use a water-soluble glue! My own preference is for GRP, since it is light, imparts great strength, and is quite watertight – foam, particularly the white variety, *will* absorb water, and takes a long time to dry out. The disadvantage of using GRP is that the surface needs quite a bit of rubbing down afterwards to get it smooth.

Really lightweight floats can be best made from blue foam, with

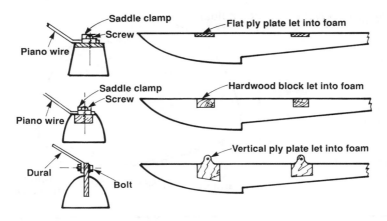

Fig. 12.7 Float attachment points

Bigfoot, a two-metre, Supre Tigre 90 powered glider tug, converted to floats. The latter have white foam cores, skinned with GRP. The model is an own-design.

Flat ply plate

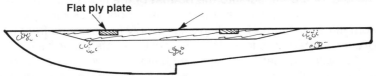

Fig. 12.8 Spar reinforcing

a strengthening strip set into the top, a plywood keel set into the bottom from the bow back to the step, the whole being painted or covered with film. My personal feeling is that this kind of float should be reserved for the smaller models, where light wing-loading is important – such models will land relatively slowly, so there will be no great strength needed. On the larger and heavier planes, a less-than-perfect landing can impose quite high loads on the floats.

If you decide to use V-bottomed floats, which do make landings

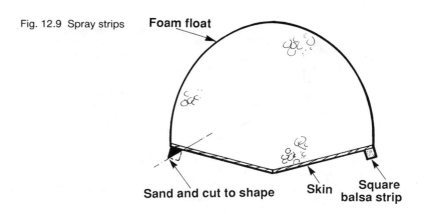

Fig. 12.9 Spray strips **Foam float**

Sand and cut to shape   **Skin**   **Square balsa strip**

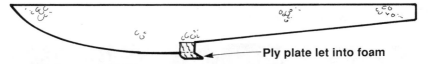

Ply plate let into foam

Fig. 12.10 Dagger plate

a lot smoother, particularly on the heavier models, you will find that they throw a lot of spray up their own sides, especially during take-off. The answer is to add spray-strips, as shown (Fig. 12.9). Simple pieces of triangular balsa glued to the bottom are most effective. You may find that a model fitted with flat-bottomed floats will skate sideways when you try to turn it. Dagger-plates, which work like the keel of a boat, set into the bottom of the floats will help here (Fig. 12.10). Difficulties in making the model track straight can sometimes be cured by adding narrow ply keels on the front half of each float – this also helps to protect the floats during beaching.

You will find that the floats may have an effect on handling in the air, too. The top of the float should be parallel to the chord line of the wing, to start with (don't forget that the undersurface of a 'flat-bottomed' aerofoil such as Clark Y, is not the aerodynamic chord line!). If snaking occurs at speed, it may be necessary to add some area to the fin – usually by means of a sub-fin under the fuselage. You can add water rudders, too.

Cowls
If you are building from a plan, or to your own design, it is often impossible to find a suitable cowl in the model shops, and so it becomes necessary to carve one from thick – and expensive –

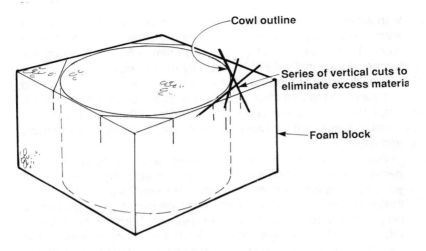

Fig. 12.11 Cutting foam block for round cowl

balsa wood. This, of course, is the time-honoured and traditional method, and is still perfectly good today. However, for really complex cowls there is a better way.

If you work with foam, you will find that, just as with wood, you will have lots of pieces left over. Start a scrap box for these off-cuts. They will come in very handy at times. This is one such occasion, because you will often find enough pieces in your box to make an entire cowl. The cost is therefore negligible.

Undoubtedly the easiest type of cowl to make is the radial variety, as found on many WWI planes. Make up a block of blue foam, large enough to carve the cowl from in one piece (don't forget to plan the glue lines, as usual). Cut the ends square with the HWC, and then draw the circle representing the outside diameter of the cowl on one end. There are several ways of cutting it out. The first is to use a fine-toothed saw or long cutter blade, and cut all the angles until the foam approximates to a circular form (Fig. 12.11). Then go to work with the sanding block.

The second way is again to cut all the angles, but then drill a central hole and tack-glue a length of dowel through it. One end goes in the chuck of the electric drill, which is held in a support. It is now quite easy, using a sharp wood-worker's chisel and the sanding block, to turn the cowl as if on a lathe.

Covering this kind of cowl can be as simple or as sophisticated as you choose. A paint job, for light weight is fine – but check the paint on a scrap of foam first! Trying pieces of nylon stocking smeared with several coats of diluted white glue is another method, or the same nylon may be used with epoxy glue, made nice and liquid with a hair-dryer or heat-gun. Iron-on film is fine, but watch the temperature. Finally, GRP is probably the strongest covering, but use bi-directional cloth, and fairly thin cloth at that, to go round the curves. Don't hesitate to cut darts in the cloth if it will not lay flat; cover with several pieces if necessary. When it is dry, fill the raised edges of the joins with 'hard' Plastic Padding, or equivalent, and rub down.

Where in-line cowls are concerned, a bit more planning is necessary. Most models require down- or side-thrust, or both. If you make the cowl before the plane has been flown, and then find that you need several degrees of engine offset, your spinner or prop-nut will be off-centre in the cowl, which spoils the appearance. A much better system is to finish the rest of the model, get the centre of gravity in the right place by using temporary weights, and fly it. Trim the model out, paying particular attention to getting the engine thrust-line right, and only then build and fit the cowl, incorporating any adjustments you have made.

On the majority of models the engine-bay set-up consists of a firewall with built-in wooden bearers poking out of it, or a commercial motor mount bolted onto it. The method of building your cowling is the same in both cases. First, cut a 2mm ply disc, the same size as the spinner backplate, and spot-glue it to the spinner. Use Clingfilm and adhesive tape to protect the edge of the firewall and the front part of the fuselage. Now cut blue foam blocks to fill the entire area between the firewall and the ply disc, but do not glue anything at this stage (Fig. 12.12). All this is done with the engine in place, which will mean carving out the inside of some of the blocks, to clear protruding parts, such as the carburetter, cylinder-head and silencer. The blocks will of course lie proud of the fuselage, to allow for carving. When you have got all the blocks in place, plan the glue lines carefully – I cannot insist enough on this point. If you do not do so, you will have trouble when it comes to finishing. Then glue the blocks together, and spot-glue them very, very lightly to the spinner disc and the firewall. Depending on the configuration of the cowl, it may be a good idea to remove the engine bearer bolts, degrease the lugs with some acetone, and spot-glue the engine to the bearers with two tiny drops of cyanoacrylate, to make its removal easier.

When everything is ready, out with the carving tools and sanding blocks and reduce the block to its final shape. Do not forget to

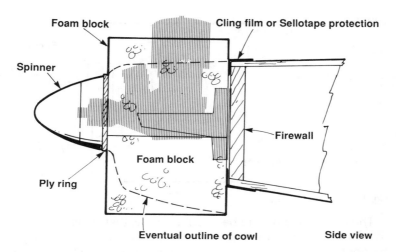

Foam block

Cling film or Sellotape protection

Spinner

Firewall

Ply ring

Foam block

Eventual outline of cowl

Side view

Fig. 12.12 Complex cowl

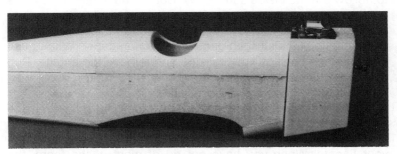

These blocks have been stuck together with Gudy O, to form the cowl. They have not yet been fixed to the fuselage.

The blocks have been cut and sanded to fair nicely into the lines of the fuselage.

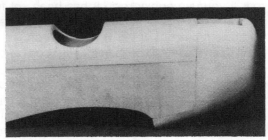

make allowances for the thickness of the skin to be used. The lines of the fuselage and spinner are carefully followed in the final sanding process, to get smooth transition and blending contours. You can use templates and the big outside calipers, but most often, eyeballing will be sufficient (Fig. 12.13).

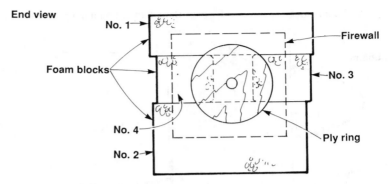

End view

No. 1

Firewall

Foam blocks

No. 3

No. 4

No. 2

Ply ring

Fig. 12.13 Complex cowl

The final shape having been obtained, all that remains to do is to skin the cowl. In the case of a complicated shape, it may just be possible to use the foam, with a coat of paint, if it is possible to hollow out the inside sufficiently. But the best method is glass cloth and epoxy glue, or resin. Be careful not to allow the resin to run into the space between the ply disc and the spinner, or into the engine – block all such gaps with kitchen paper. When quite dry, prise the cowl off the fuselage and remove the engine. Rub down the GRP cowl surface with emery paper, used wet, eliminating any imperfections with filler.

You still have the remains of the foam blocks inside. Now is the time to remove them. With a chisel or knife, dig out as much as you can – be careful, you will be surprised at how hard it is. Watch your fingers! When you have got rid of most of the foam, the remainder can be dissolved with a little acetone, but make sure that if you use epoxy resin it has been set for at least 48 hours before doing this, otherwise the acetone may soften the GRP – and nine times out of ten, it will stay soft!

All that remains to do is paint your cowl and fix it in place on the fuselage.

Perhaps you require several identical cowls – for a club project, for instance. In this case, give the foam a thin skinning of epoxy and glass cloth, remove it, rub down, fill, paint, and generally obtain a really good finish. Then wax it several times, with a non-silicone release wax, and make a female mould. You can use polyester resin for this, since the foam is now protected from it by the initial skin, and polyester is a lot cheaper than epoxy. It can be found on the car accessory shelves of DIY shops. Do not carry out this operation in the house, the smell is very strong, obnoxious and lingering! Build up the mould to a good thickness, at least 3mm, and let it dry for at least 48 hours – polyester mouldings contract quite a lot during polymerisation. This mould can now be used to make as many cowls as you need, using the normal GRP laying-up process.

Naturally, this method is not limited to making cowls. Many accessories can be made in the same way. Wheel spats, gun blisters, wing root fillets and canopies, for example.

Canopies

It may surprise some people to find canopies mentioned in connection with foam techniques. There are two useful methods. One is to carve a canopy from blue foam, skin it with GRP, and then paint it (Fig. 12.14). The best colours are blue, and surprisingly, metallic bronze. The latter, on a large, white, glider fuselage, looks really attractive.

The second method is to make the foam canopy in the same way, but to give it a really thick skin of GRP, rub down and fill until the finish is quite impeccable, and then use this as a plug to thermo-form a transparent plastic canopy. This latter process falls

A four-metre glider, with a bronze-painted GRP canopy which was made with a foam core.

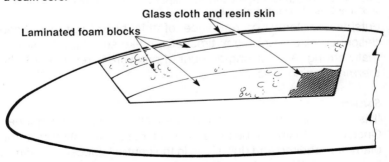

Fig. 12.14 Foam canopy

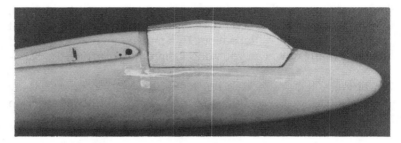

The block of blue foam which will eventually form the basis for the canopy on this Pilatus B4. Rough cutting, with the mini-HWC, has already been carried out.

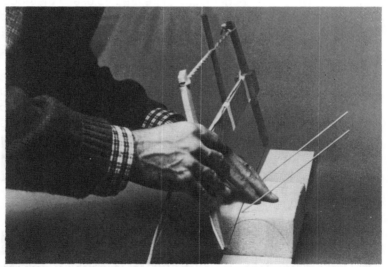

Using bamboo skewers as cutting guides, the rounded, upper part of the canopy is about to be cut roughly to shape. This avoids fastidious cutting, and shavings all over the place!

outside the terms of reference of this book, but has been described elsewhere many times. Do make sure that the skin is really strong. A surprising amount of pressure is required for the thermo-forming process.

Spinners

It is not always possible to find a suitable commercial spinner. Once again, foam can be used. First cut out a 2mm ply disc of the diameter required and drill a hole in the centre to accept a 4–5mm bolt and nut. Glue a block of blue foam onto the disc, hold the bolt in the chuck of an electric drill, and turn and sand the spinner to

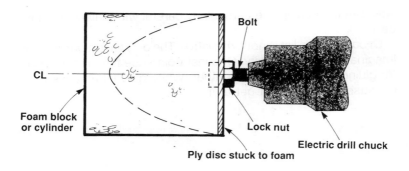

Bolt

CL

Foam block
or cylinder

Lock nut

Electric drill chuck

Ply disc stuck to foam

Fig. 12.15 Foam spinner

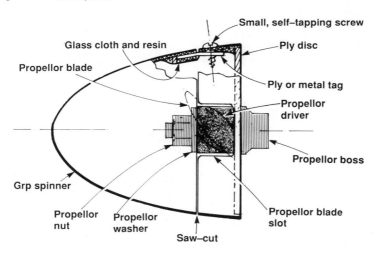

Small, self–tapping screw

Glass cloth and resin

Ply disc

Propellor blade

Ply or metal tag

Propellor
driver

Propellor boss

Grp spinner

Propellor blade
slot

Propellor
nut

Propellor
washer

Saw–cut

Fig. 12.16 Spinner fixing

the shape required (Fig. 12.15). For electric models the skin can
be a coat of paint, or nylon and glue, applied very thinly, to save
weight. Otherwise, epoxy should be used, and it will be necessary
to balance the spinner afterwards by adding small pieces of glass
cloth and epoxy glue at the appropriate places inside the cone
(Fig. 12.16). Use a sensitive balancing device, and it is a good idea
to balance the spinner and the prop to be used as one whole unit.

On models which turn out to be tail-heavy – it happens to the
best of us! – a good trick is to build up the layers of GRP inside
the cone until the centre of gravity is in the right place. Of course,
there is a limit to the amount of weight that can be added in this

way, but it can help. Be particularly careful with balancing in this case.

Of course, this list is not exhaustive. The only limitations are your imagination and ingenuity. One last point: use five-minute epoxy for gluing blocks of foam together. White glue takes days to set because the air cannot get to it.

13 REPAIRS

Damage to wings

One of the objections to the use of foam in model planes is that they are difficult to repair in the event of damage. In fact, this is far from the case, and I personally would much prefer to repair a broken foam wing than one built in the traditional manner.

Most repairs will be to wings, since this is probably the most vulnerable part of a model, liable to attacks by trees, bushes, fence-posts, large stones, and more besides! Almost invariably it is the leading edge that gets crushed in these conditions, so we will deal with that, first. We have to repair a typical, foam core wing, skinned with obechi and with an added LE spar (Fig. 13.1). An obstruction has bitten about 2in. into the wing. The first thing to do is to inspect the area, and see how far back it is necessary to

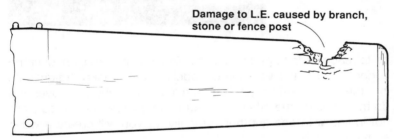

Damage to L.E. caused by branch, stone or fence post

Fig. 13.1 Damage to leading edge

This damaged Moonraker wing looks pretty bad, but repair is simple.

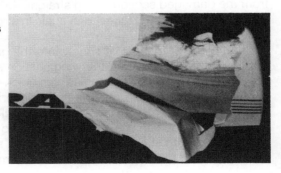

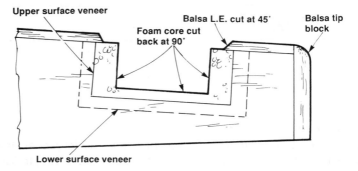

Upper surface veneer

Balsa L.E. cut at 45°

Balsa tip block

Foam core cut back at 90°

Lower surface veneer

Fig. 13.2 Cutting away veneer for repair

The damaged area has been cut away and the repair can now start.

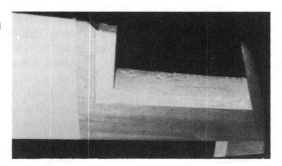

go to reach undamaged structure. Mark out this area, uncover the surface, and, with a very sharp modelling knife, make straight cuts into the skin, prising it gently off the foam. Turn the wing over and do the same on the other side, but try to ensure that the cuts are not in line with one another vertically, or you will create a weak spot (Fig. 13.2).

Next, cut away the LE spar a couple of inches back on each side from the damaged section, using straight, 45 degree cuts. Finally cut away the damaged foam core, again in straight lines. The area is now ready for repair.

Cut a piece of foam to fit snugly into the gap you have made, but it must be thicker than the wing section and overhanging at the LE (Fig. 13.3). Glue this in place with quick-setting epoxy. Now carefully cut this down until it is quite close to the original core section, and finish off with small sanding blocks covered with 400 grade emery. You can use a small HWC to do this, protecting the wing surface with sticky tape. When you are satisfied with the fit and shape, cut the upper and lower replacement skin parts, and

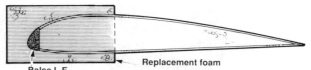

Balsa L.E. Replacement foam

N.B. The replacement foam block can be cut down almost to the final size by running the HWC over the wing surface

Fig. 13.3 Fitting replacement foam block

Here the foam insert has been glued in place and shaped to match the original.

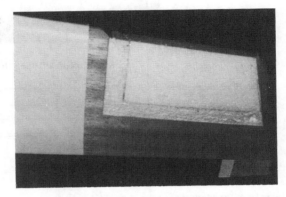

The obechi skin replacements have been cut to size, glued in place and sanded down. All that remains to do is to fit and glue the leading edge.

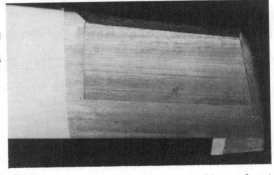

glue them in place. They can be held down with a small bag of wet sand or sticky tape during the drying process. When dry, sand them flush with the rest of the surface, and also true-up the area where the replacement LE spar is to be fitted. This latter is then cut to shape, glued into place, sanded down, and the repair is almost finished. All you now have to do is re-cover the area. Carried out in this way, the repaired section of the wing will be as strong as the rest.

Another frequent cause of damage is the dreaded one-wing-low landing, where the tip of one wing-panel hits the ground first,

The repaired wing, as good as new.

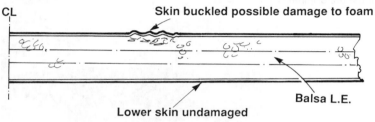

CL

Skin buckled possible damage to foam

Balsa L.E.

Lower skin undamaged

Fig. 13.4 Buckled wing skin

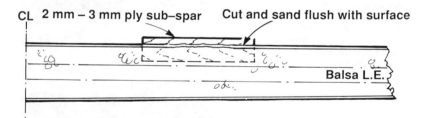

CL **2 mm – 3 mm ply sub–spar** **Cut and sand flush with surface**

Balsa L.E.

Fig. 13.5 Let-in spar repair (brown paper or card skin)

absorbing all the impact and bending to the point where it buckles. What has happened is that the lower skin is placed under great tension, the upper under compression, and the foam core allows it to bend to the point of rupture (Fig. 13.4). The repair depends on the type of structure used. On brown-paper and card skinned wings, the easiest repair is to cut a rectangular piece out of the skin, dig a clean channel into the foam, and glue a plywood spar into place, its length being such that it ends 3–4in. on either side of the buckled area. This sort of repair seems very simple, but is actually very efficient (Fig. 13.5).

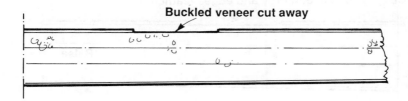

Buckled veneer cut away

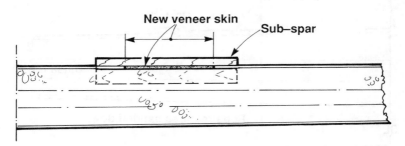

New veneer skin

Sub–spar

Fig. 13.6 Let-in spar repair (balsa or obechi skin)

On a balsa- or obechi-skinned wing, you will have to carefully remove the buckled area for about 3in. on either side, let in a spar as before, and then re-skin (Fig. 13.6). If you are lucky, this will only be necessary on one surface, depending on the amount of buckling.

GRP repairs

If you have a wing with a glass cloth reinforcing, there is a very simple method of repair. Drill a series of 1mm holes through the skin all over the damaged area. Now hold the wing perfectly flat, and drop very liquid cyanoacrylate glue into the holes. This will bond the skin to the glass reinforcing; and the repair is done. However, a word of warning. Make sure that the glue goes into the area where the glass cloth is below the skin, and not where there is foam directly below it, or the glue will attack the foam.

Repairs to a foam-core wing with a GRP skin are very similar. The process is the same up to the replacement of the skin. At this point, you have to carefully feather the edges of the good parts on either side, lay-up glass cloth and resin over the exposed foam, so that it overlaps onto these feathered edges, and when it has set rub it down with wet-and-dry paper, used wet, until the repair is blended into the rest of the surface (Fig. 13.7). It takes quite a bit of elbow-grease, but is a much better option than throwing the

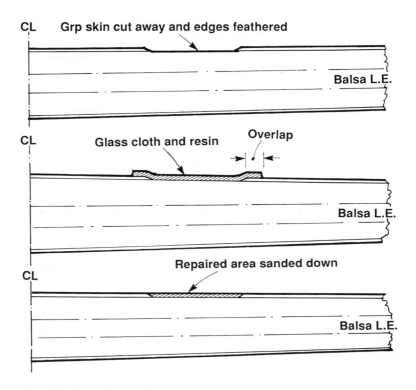

CL   **Grp skin cut away and edges feathered**

Balsa L.E.

CL   **Glass cloth and resin**   **Overlap**

Balsa L.E.

Repaired area sanded down

CL

Balsa L.E.

Fig. 13.7 Glass wing repair

wing away. It is a good idea to use a couple of lengths of carbon or Kevlar tow in the repair.

Fractures

From time to time a wing gets broken completely in two! Not to worry, this is very often quite repairable. Try fitting the two parts back together. This is sometimes possible if the crash has not torn away too much skin or foam. If it looks feasible, the first thing to do is to glue the two halves together, using epoxy on the foam core. The greatest difficult here lies in keeping the two broken ends in contact whilst the glue sets. The solution is to drill four 2mm holes, two on each side of the break and about 3in. back from it. Push bamboo skewers through these holes, apply the glue to the core, fit the two parts together, and then use small elastic bands around the skewers, above and below the panel, to create a joint which is under constant pressure while the glue sets (Fig. 13.8). Subsequently, cut away and replace the damaged skins and LE

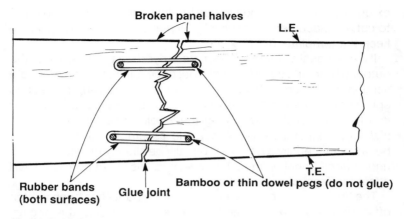

Fig. 13.8 Joining halves of broken wing panel

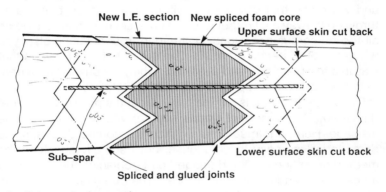

1. Cut away broken section
2. Cut and glue in place new foam section
3. Shape new foam section
4. Let in ply sub–spar
5. Replace skin sections
6. Replace L.E. section
7. Sand flush and re–cover

Fig. 13.9 Replacing broken wing section

spar as before.

If the break is such that you cannot reasonably fit the two broken parts together, more drastic surgery is called for. First, you may be able to get away with cutting out a very short length of the panel with perfectly straight and vertical cuts. Take off the upper and lower skins for 3in. back on each side. Cut a piece of foam to replace the missing core, and glue it in place, taking great care not to introduce a twist or warp into the panel! Cut and sand this block to the original core section, let in small ply spars as before, and re-skin (Fig. 13.9). If the section that has to be cut away is more extensive, it is a good idea to use the original templates and HWC to cut a replacement part, which will make the job easier (you did keep the template, didn't you!).

If a great deal of wing has been destroyed – say, one-third of the outboard end, the easiest solution is, once again, to cut a new core section, make a neat V-cut in the end of the old wing panel, and splice this section to it. Then continue the process as before. This is a lot cheaper than replacing the whole panel. If you do this, always be careful to re-balance the assembled plane laterally, because the repaired panel will usually be slightly heavier than the undamaged panel on the other side, and this, if not corrected, will affect the flight characteristics.

The final case, of course, is when a wing panel has been written off completely – a comparatively rare event. Using the original templates, build a complete new panel! It is relatively quick to do, and will mean that your model will fly again; much better than throwing it away as, I regret to say, I have seen enthusiasts do on all-too-numerous occasions. Quite apart from anything else, you will get a lot of personal satisfaction out of restoring a wing that was in a terrible mess, and a real kick when the others find it hard to believe that it is a repair, and not an entirely new wing!

Of course, the wing is not the only part of the plane that can get damaged. The same techniques apply if you use foam for the fuselage. Here, it is much more difficult to go into details, since damage is less easy to categorise, but generally speaking the method of cutting out the damaged part, replacing the foam with a fresh piece and re-skinning applies. The true answer to all this, of course, is not to crash them!

14 AEROFOILS

Selection

Since this book is aimed, in part, at beginners who want to try their hand at making foam cores for wings, it is necessary to provide some aerofoil sections, since without them, they will not be able to cut any cores! Of course, as already mentioned, you can draw round the wing section of a broken model, and there are always plans to be bought and copied. However, a selection of basic sections, to cover the most usual types of models, can only provide a further encouragement to have a go.

The difficulty is in selecting a small number from the several hundred available. No-one will argue with the first choice, which is the old, but still reliable Clark Y, that standby of modellers all over the world for the past 50–60 years, which still takes some beating for general purpose flying. Contrary to certain suggestions, the Clark Y *will* fly inverted, if correctly set-up!

Plotting the section

How do we go about drawing up an aerofoil? Use the tables of ordinates listed at the end of this chapter, and it is quite simple. Let's go back to Chapter 3 and our 50 × 7in. trainer wing. We require a 7in. chord aerofoil to be developed from the Clark Y ordinate table. If you look at this table, you will see that there are three columns, the first marked *Station*, the second *Upper* and the third *Lower*.

The first column goes from 0 to 100, and, when multiplied by the chord width chosen – 7in. in this case – will tell us where to use the results of the other two columns along the chord line. Multiplying the other two columns by seven will give us the thickness of the aerofoil, above and below the chord line, at the increasing distances given in the first column. That sounds rather complicated, but will become quite clear when you start drawing. When you have finished the multiplication, you will find that for exact dimensions you will need to move the decimal point two places to the left in every case.

Having obtained the appropriate figures, we now need to

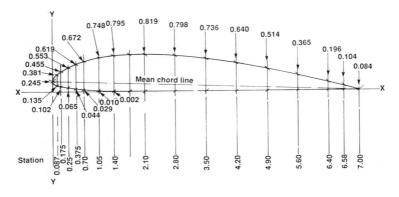

Fig. 14.1 Plotting and drawing an airfoil

transform them into the required aerofoil. There are two ways of doing this; either draw the section on paper (squared millimetre paper is a great help here) and then transfer it to the template material, or draw it directly on the ply or whatever. The second solution is probably better, since there is no chance of distortion in the transfer process. Whichever you use, the principle is the same. Let's take a look at drawing directly on the template material.

First draw two axes, *X* horizontally and *Y* vertically. The intersection point is *O*, and it is from here that you mark off, along *X*, the figures you have calculated under *Station*. Draw very fine vertical lines through each of these points, and write-in the figures, because it is all too easy to make mistakes if you don't, and very time-consuming and annoying to retrace all the steps to find out where you went wrong (Fig. 14.1).

There are two common ways of giving the ordinates. In the majority of cases, the mean chord line coincides with the *X* axis. In this case, the points that should occur below the line will have a minus sign in front of them (see the NACA 2412 table). However, some tables are published in such a way that the points all occur above the *X* axis, and the mean chord line is thus at an angle to it (see the Clark Y table). In this case there are no minus signs in the *Lower* column. It is quite obvious which system is which.

You now mark off the distances given in the *Upper* column, as shown. Work with a very fine pencil point, and as accurately as possible, but don't hesitate to round off the figures – there is just no way that you can draw to three places of decimals! When you have got all the upper marks in, go back to the top of the column, and do the same thing for the *Lower* figures.

By drawing lines between the marks you have made, you will end up with an aerofoil section. You should aim to do this as accurately as possible, the performance of the resulting wing will depend, within limits, on how well this is done. Drawing the curve can be done in several ways. The traditional one is to use a set of French curves. Secondly, you can now buy rubber rulers, with a segmented metal insert, which can be bent into curves, and which will stay in place until re-bent. Or you can follow my system, which is to rest your wrist on the work surface, inside the curve to be drawn, and lightly sketch, freehand, the line joining the points. You will see that by resting your wrist on the surface, your hand is working rather like the arm of a compass, and it is possible to draw quite accurate curves. When the light pencil strokes are correct, go over it more heavily. Repeat for the other side. All that remains to be done is to cut it out, as explained in Chapter 3.

If, when joining the points, you find that one of them is a bit out, go back and check your calculations. You may have made a mistake. (Be sure to check the *Station* position as well as the *Upper* or *Lower*.) If these are correct, you have come across something which does occur from time to time; a mistake in the table, possibly a printing error. Ignore this 'rogue' point, continuing your line in a smooth curve through the two adjacent points.

Aerofoil choices

Precisely what can the Clark Y aerofoil be used for? The first example is our trainer, for 2.5–5cc motors. It can be used on quite a few scale models, particularly of the high-wing variety, and on primary gliders and slope soarers. It really is a most versatile aerofoil.

The second choice is one which will allow semi-beginners – those who can already fly a basic trainer – to build something a little more responsive. This is the NACA 2412, which, again, is not modern, but which, like the Clark Y, has proved its value over a long period and many models. Commonly called a semi-symmetrical section, it allows all basic aerobatics, and will fly inverted with only a little 'down' on the elevator. Since it has 12 per cent thickness/chord ratio there is no chance of structural weakness; low-speed characteristics are good – providing the model is not too heavy – and it has a wide speed range. In addition, it is suitable for both power models and gliders.

However, where aerobatic gliders, or rather slope-soarers, are concerned, a better choice would probably be the Eppler 374, which has graced many models in recent years. And not only is it a good aerobatic section, it will also allow fairly lightly-loaded models to stay up when the wind drops. Whilst it has a reasonable speed range, it will not whistle around like some, so it is quite suitable for a modeller who has got the basic aerobatics under his belt, and who wants something a little more exciting. Experimenters may want to try a wing with 10 degrees of sweep-back on the leading edge. The result is a model that can be slowed right down to walking pace in a light wind, without stalling, which makes it easier to land on slopes where the landing area is very limited in size. Despite this, the aerobatic capacity remains intact.

For big gliders of above 100in. span, there are two very good aerofoils, the Wortmann Fx 60–126 and the Eppler 212, the latter being a relatively recent development. It is excellent on the medium-size models too, from 80in. up, but above 120–130in. the Wortmann comes into its own. Both were designed for use on the tips of full-sized gliders, are efficient at the Reynolds numbers at which we fly, and have been adopted by modellers as all-purpose sections for large, scale models.

You will see that there is a big difference between the ordinate tables for these two and those for the others already mentioned. In the first place, there are far more numbers, because they are fairly modern designs, calculated on computers, and the extra numbers are included to make it possible to draw more accurate sections. This makes drawing them slightly more complicated. Let's take the Eppler first: you will notice that there are only two columns which are used to draw the section, the first one being merely the number of each station. The second table gives these positions, but in a different manner – it starts at the tip of the trailing edge, goes forward, up over the upper surface, turns around between Nos. 31 and 32 and comes back along the bottom surface, arriving at the departure point with No. 60. The stations are irregular, due to the design method, but are calculated in the same way, by multiplying the figures by the required chord-width.

The Wortmann is different again. The first column gives the stations, but there are 100 of them, and they are not positioned evenly (again for design considerations). The other two columns, in the table shown, are used in the same way as the Clark Y and NACA sections, but this is an exception. Most Wortmann ordinates are given in the same way as the Eppler.

For out-and-out aerobatics with a power model, especially if it is built fairly lightly, a most suitable section is the NACA 63 3 018. This is a section with a relative thickness of 18 per cent, which means that it will not accelerate a great deal in downwards manoeuvres, and which has a very gentle stall. It is fully symmetrical, so will fly as well inverted as right-side-up. It is ideal for the new style Aresti programme, where the manoeuvres have to be carried out in a limited space, instead of the older, missile-trajectory style manoeuvres.

Finally comes the NACA 0009. This is a fairly thin, symmetrical section, which has become extremely popular for use on tail-planes. There is a very good reason for this; a flat-plate tailplane has a quite violent reaction as soon as the elevator is deflected (depending exactly, of course, on the other design parameters of the model). The 0009 has a much softer reaction around the zero position, hardening up progressively as it is deflected further. This means that a model equipped with this type of tailplane can be flown more smoothly. For this reason it is almost essential on T-tails fitted to large sailplanes. In addition, the drag at progressive angles of incidence is less than for the same angle with a flat plate, which, of course, makes it more efficient. The disadvantage is that it requires more work to construct than a flat plate, but, if you use the newly-discovered techniques of working with foam, you can very easily cut a foam core and skin it with balsa – 1mm is thick enough, given the very short span of most tailplanes – which makes construction very simple. If weight is a large consideration, and it usually is on tailplanes, then it is quite simple to drill 2in. holes in the core before skinning, to lighten it.

Inevitably, the selection of aerofoil sections given is, in the first place, very limited, and, in the second, a personal choice. There will no doubt be readers who want something else, or who do not agree with my choice. To those in the first category I would say, hunt around, there are many publications which supply aerofoil sections, it is up to you now to find them. This book is about foam construction, not aerodynamics. Over the past few years I have built up a collection of over two hundred different sections. A good source is the index to Martin Simons' book 'Model Aircraft Aero-dynamics', which contains well over 100 sections.

As for those who do not agree with my choice, I can only say that these are aerofoils I have used myself in some numbers over the years; and whatever else one can say about them, they do work. My experience also tells me that where five modellers are collected together to discuss one model, they will advocate five different aerofoils for it, usually vociferously!

Be that as it may, you now have a small selection of tables that you can use to cut your teeth on, plus whatever you may have already found. This nucleus will serve as a starting point for your collection.

Clark Y

Station	Upper	Lower
0	3.5	3.5
1.25	5.45	1.93
2.5	6.5	1.47
5	7.9	0.93
7.5	8.85	0.63
10	9.6	0.42
15	10.69	0.15
20	11.36	0.03
30	11.7	0.00
40	11.4	0.00
50	10.52	0.00
60	9.15	0.00
70	7.35	0.00
80	5.22	0.00
90	2.8	0.00
95	1.49	0.00
100	0.12	0.00

Figures developed for 7in. chord

Station	Upper	Lower
0	0.24	0.24
0.08	0.38	0.13
0.17	0.45	0.10
0.25	0.55	0.06
0.37	0.61	0.04
0.70	0.67	0.03
1.05	0.75	0.01
1.40	0.80	0.00
2.10	0.81	0.00
2.80	0.80	0.00
3.50	0.73	0.00
4.20	0.64	0.00
4.90	0.51	0.00
5.60	0.36	0.00
6.40	0.19	0.00
6.58	0.10	0.00
7.00	0.08	0.00

NACA 2412

Station	Upper	Lower
0	–	0
1.25	2.15	−1.65
2.5	2.99	−2.27
5.0	4.13	−3.01
7.5	4.96	−3.46
10	5.63	−3.75
15	6.61	−4.10
20	7.26	−4.23
25	7.67	−4.22
30	7.88	−4.12
40	7.80	−3.80
50	7.24	−3.34
60	6.36	−2.76
70	5.18	−2.14
80	3.75	−1.50
90	2.08	−0.82
95	1.14	−0.48
100	0	0

Wortmann FX 60–126

Station	Upper	Lower	Station	Upper	Lower
.000	.000	.000	49.997	8.425	−1.421
.102	.675	−.301	53.274	8.118	−1.036
.422	1.349	−.641	56.525	7.781	−.653
.960	2.096	−1.012	57.750	7.402	−.298
1.702	2.802	−1.404	62.938	6.994	.029
2.650	3.493	−1.792	66.074	6.549	.307
3.802	4.174	−2.132	69.133	6.082	.547
5.158	4.808	−2.482	72.115	5.589	.741
6.694	5.457	−2.671	74.995	5.084	.897
8.422	6.021	−3.045	77.773	4.567	1.006
10.330	6.585	−3.262	80.435	4.055	1.073
12.403	7.077	−3.465	82.970	3.552	1.093
14.643	7.555	−3.598	87.590	2.611	1.022
17.037	7.958	−3.707	89.644	2.181	.944
19.558	8.327	−3.746	91.571	1.777	.845
22.221	8.615	−3.751	93.299	1.412	.732
24.998	8.859	−3.683	94.848	1.084	.610
27.891	9.019	−3.574	96.192	.798	.483
30.861	9.130	−3.392	97.344	.554	.357
33.933	9.160	−3.167	98.291	.353	.239
37.056	9.138	−2.877	99.034	.198	.146
40.243	9.041	−2.553	99.571	.088	.068
43.469	8.893	−2.188	99.891	.024	.014
46.733	8.679	−1.814	100.00	.0000	.00000

NACA 0009

Station	Upper	Lower
0.00	0.00	0.00
0.20	0.49	0.49
0.40	0.82	0.82
0.60	1.01	1.01
0.80	1.17	1.17
1.25	1.42	1.42
2.50	1.96	1.96
5.00	2.66	2.66
7.50	3.15	3.15
10.0	3.51	3.51
15.0	4.01	4.01
20.0	4.30	4.30
25.0	4.45	4.45
30.0	4.50	4.50
40.0	4.35	4.35
50.0	3.97	3.97
60.0	3.42	3.42
70.0	2.75	2.75
80.0	1.96	1.96
90.0	1.08	1.08
95.0	0.60	0.60
100	0.09	0.09

Eppler 212

Station	Upper	Lower	Station	Upper	Lower
0	100.0	0.00			
1	99.676	.092	31	.032	.224
2	98.759	.372	32	.122	−.398
3	97.346	.803	33	.800	−.970
4	95.472	1.307	34	1.984	−1.532
5	93.124	1.844	35	3.648	−2.045
6	90.316	2.418	36	5.780	−2.486
7	87.085	3.023	37	8.363	−2.840
8	83.474	3.645	38	11.379	−3.097
9	79.525	4.269	39	14.808	−3.252
10	75.283	4.881	40	18.621	−3.301
11	70.796	5.465	41	22.790	−3.248
12	66.112	6.008	42	27.280	−3.099
13	61.282	6.496	43	32.051	−2.861
14	56.355	6.915	44	37.059	−2.548
15	51.383	7.256	45	42.257	−2.175
16	46.416	7.507	46	47.590	−1.759
17	41.502	7.660	47	53.003	−1.320
18	36.689	7.708	48	58.434	−.878
19	32.023	7.647	49	63.819	−.452
20	27.548	7.473	50	69.090	−.063
21	23.303	7.188	51	74.179	.271
22	19.326	6.794	52	79.016	.535
23	15.651	6.295	53	83.528	.713
24	12.309	5.701	54	87.643	.794
25	9.327	5.023	55	91.284	.776
26	6.729	4.275	56	94.382	.659
27	4.534	3.473	57	96.851	.458
28	2.578	2.636	58	98.615	.231
29	1.410	1.790	59	99.657	.061
30	.499	.967	60	100.000	.000

Eppler 374

Station	Upper	Lower
0	0	0
1.25	1.4	1.1
2.5	2.2	1.5
5.0	3.4	2.0
7.5	4.2	2.4
10	4.9	2.7
15	5.9	3.0
20	6.6	3.1
25	7.2	3.2
30	7.5	3.3
40	7.7	3.2
50	7.1	2.9
60	6.0	2.6
70	4.6	2.2
80	3.1	1.5
90	1.6	0.8
95	0.9	0.4
100	0	0

INDEX